Astrological

Counselling

Astrological

Counselling

A basic guide to astrological themes in person–to–person relationships

Christina Rose

The Wessex Astrologer

Published in 2024 by
The Wessex Astrologer Ltd
PO Box 9307
Swanage
BH19 9BF

For a full list of our titles go to www.wessexastrologer.com

Copyright © The Estate of Christina Rose 1982

The Estate of Christina Rose asserts the moral right of Christina Rose to be identified as the author of this work

Cover design by Fiona Bowring

A catalogue record for this book is available at The British Library

ISBN 9781916625198

originally published in 1982 by The Aquarian Press
ISBN 085030301X

No part of this book may be reproduced or used in any form or by any means without the written permission of the publisher.
A reviewer may quote brief passages.

CONTENTS

	Introduction	9

PART 1: BASIC PERSPECTIVES

1.	Astrology in Transition	15
2.	The Universe and the Individual	19
3.	The Nature of Astrological Counselling	23
4.	The Birth Chart as a Guide in our Development	29

PART 2: THE BIRTH CHART

5.	The Planets and Angles in Counselling	35
6.	The Cycle of the Zodiac and the Elements	61
7.	Houses and Aspects	81
8.	Key Points: Progressions, Transits and Major Cycles	101

PART 3: THE ASTROLOGER'S FRAMEWORK: THE CLIENT'S NEEDS

9.	First Steps to Consultation	131
10.	Interpretation and Counselling	135
11.	Finding Solutions to Problems	141
12.	Conclusion	151
	Appendix I: Recommended Reading	155
	Index	157

ACKNOWLEDGEMENTS

Permission to use copyright material from the following works is gratefully acknowledged as follows:

To William Heinemann Ltd and to Laurence Pollinger Ltd and to the Estate of Frieda Lawrence Ravagli for an extract from 'Surgery for the Novel – or A Bomb' by D. H. Lawrence, from *Phoenix: The Posthumous Papers of D. H. Lawrence*, edited by Edward McDonald, copyright 1936 by Frieda Lawrence. Copyright renewed 1964 by the Estate of the late Frieda Lawrence. Reprinted by permission of Viking Penguin Inc., New York.

To Dane Rudhyar for permission to quote from *The Practice of Astrology*, published by Penguin Books Inc. 1968.

To Alexander Ruperti for permission to quote from *Cycles of Becoming : The Planetary Pattern of Growth*, published 1978 by CRCS Publications, Nevada, USA.

To June Singer for permission to quote from *Androgyny: Towards a New Theory of Sexuality*, published by Routledge and Kegan Paul Ltd, 1976.

To Martin Goodsell for assistance with diagrams and Karen Chapman for planetary and zodiac symbols.

Especially to all those people (whose names have been altered for reasons of confidentiality) who have permitted extracts from their conversations with the author to be reproduced, together with information concerning their birth charts.

For
E. M. R.

If the astrologer thinks he merely gives bits of information and then is through with the whole thing, he is greatly mistaken. He has established a relationship.

DANE RUDHYAR

INTRODUCTION

Astrology is increasingly being turned to as a path of very deep significance by those who seek clarification and purpose amid the uncertainty and confusion of their lives.

In what is frequently referred to as a 'consciousness explosion', more and more people today are concentrating on the quality, content and better management of their development through life. They want to increase their self-understanding, to be able to accept themselves more, to handle conflicts and difficulties by making sense out of them, to grasp the possible reasons for the problems or crises they meet. They also want to understand their relationship to the people with whom they live, work, or who are otherwise important to them. In order to help them with all of these things, they frequently want to talk things over with someone they feel will understand, accept and enlighten them. This may be anyone from the 'professional helper' to, indeed, the close friend around the corner; but whoever is chosen is, to the seeker, someone who is in a position, and has the ability, to help. Very frequently it is the astrologer.

When it comes to the pursuit of well-being in life, the central point of reference is the individual himself and the nature of his development, to which the astrological chart is a most insightful guide. Astrology can help pinpoint with immediacy the nature of issues arising in a person's life upon which that person may feel he needs counselling or other therapeutic guidance. Moreover, it can help identify the underlying significance endeavouring to emerge from what is experienced by the person only as a problem he would like to be rid of. When we are in difficult situations, at the core there may be something of value which can help us see things in a new light and set us on a new road. In this sense, astrology can help us look at problems and anxieties as potential challenges and opportunities.

It is by the use of astrology for trite character delineation and hard-and-fast prediction of events that the deeper meanings and understandings this time-honoured study can lead us to are being lost. Today, it is being thrown into sharp relief that astrologers are unlikely, to say the least, to be able to meet the needs of their clients as mentioned above if outmoded perceptions and practices of their subject are held intact. Parallel to this, rather than remaining solely in the role of interpreter and delivering static analyses that exclude anything the client may have to say on the matter, a great many of today's astrologers are attuning their work to, and training themselves in, several skills that will render both their understanding and translation of the birth chart a process of more worthwhile consequence. These skills range over a wide field of deeper astrological, psychological, spiritual, philosophical and psychotherapeutic understandings; but central to them all is the ability purposefully to communicate with and relate to another person who is in some way troubled, perplexed or otherwise experiencing a general search for direction in life. Not only is the astrologer a translator of chart factors, but he or she is also required to deliver that translation in ways which are appropriate to, and include, the client, his current way of being and his situation. In other words, traditional astrological interpretations are being transcended and the wider arena beyond beckons the astrologer forward as counsellor.

Addressing itself both to the general reader and the student of astrology, this book will take an overview of the main transitions now occurring in astrology that are leading to new perspectives, focusing in particular on its contemporary use as a counselling tool. The contents of the birth chart itself will also be covered in relation to how astrological counsellors regard and use it. For those who may be considering going to an astrological counsellor for consultation, information will be given on finding one who is suited to your needs and the considerations involved in choosing. The clarifications to be gained from a birth chart can often be of enormous value to those who may also be engaged in some other form of personal psychotherapeutic work, offering an adjunct from which to focus their therapy more clearly. Similarly, those working in what are generally called 'the helping professions' will find it extremely helpful to have some acquaintance with astrological principles, *if only because their clients require it of them* by wanting to discuss new awarenesses they have come to from working with their birth charts. Indeed, there is a fertile area of cross-referral now beginning to be cultivated between astrological, psychological and other practitioners who are all linked by one central purpose: that of human understanding.

For the student of astrology, it is hoped that this book may help you clarify some basic guidelines on attuning yourself to the work involved in astrological counselling. It will not be a book of set interpretations nor counselling approaches, although the 'flavour' of each may come across in the examples. However, none of these are meant to convey any definitive system or speciality of either astrology or counselling, which would be better placed in a book for the practising professional. The accent is upon the basic employment of the information derived from a birth chart, which can never be 'set' since the actual way it is experienced by the individual in his life emerges through dialogue between him and the astrological counsellor. Each person, each situation, is different.

Purely for the sake of ease, throughout the book the client will be referred to in the masculine gender and the astrological counsellor in the feminine, each to include the other (unless the discussion of a particular individual dictates otherwise).

PART 1:
BASIC PERSPECTIVES

1.
ASTROLOGY IN TRANSITION

Before looking at the present-day practice of astrological counselling, it may be helpful to connect with some of the factors that have led to its emergence, particularly if the subject is new to you. As a matter of fact (and as intimated in the Introduction), in many ways it is new to astrologers themselves, for, in scanning back (even as little as fifteen or twenty years), it is clear that the practice of astrology has undergone immense changes.

The most important features of these have been, first of all, a shift from traditional (and often extremely archaic) views and interpretations, with their talk of benevolent and malevolent stars and precise predictions of what else was in store, to a greater understanding of the fundamental *principles* or processes of life experience symbolized by planets and zodiacal signs—principles that are formative to all life and present in every human being. This has brought in its wake an increased awareness of the essential unity between man and the universe, each as a determinant in and an effect upon the other. More recently has come the growing recognition that the act of interpreting a birth chart is only of limited value unless the client can be involved in that process as well as the astrologer and can be guided into possible ways of utilizing the information derived from the chart once it has been presented to him.

To take the first of these changes, everybody knows or has heard about the usual and traditional manner of consulting an astrologer. It has been the pattern for most people to do so in an eager and excited attempt to find out if their birth chart 'rings true' and to hear what they can expect in the future. Their expectations, generally, are that they will be 'told things' and if there is a problem of current concern they tend to await an outpouring of decisions from some irrefutable cosmic oracle. All of these expectations, understandably, are in accordance with the way astrology is largely promoted in public.

The view perpetrated in this traditional astrological scheme of things has been of human beings as helpless puppets on unseen cosmic strings needing to try and maintain a control over, and defence against, what is regarded as a temperamental and unfriendly universe. For instance, its practitioners have issued avoidance instructions ('Watch out, Uranus is crossing your Mars this week so you are liable to have accidents'), classified individuals for quick disposal ('Yes, well, she's got four planets in Pisces so she's confused and over-emotional'), created the belief that a physical planet is responsible for a negative situation ('You've got Saturn in the seventh house so you won't be happy in marriage') and encouraged people to await, either in hope or dread, tangible events which are predicted exactly, but exactly, even to the day.

This might be an extreme picture for some (although of course it does still exist and sometimes takes on a character of quite singular stupidity), but it should not be allowed to cloud the fact that there are a great number (indeed, a growing number) of well-trained consultants in astrology who do not subscribe to this sort of approach but recognize that there is a deeper level of understanding to be had from astrology that reaches beyond the endless listing of character traits and the prognostication of good and bad days. These are diligent people who render intelligent and perceptive interpretations of their clients' charts along lines that can help those clients reach greater self-awareness, and this kind of astrological consultancy is of immense value.

However, from the point of view of astrological *counselling*, the gist of the matter is that, by and large, people have expected to be the entirely passive recipients of astrological pronouncements— and astrologers have complied with this expectation by affording little or no opportunity to the client to express what *his* experience of himself might be. He has not often been talked *with* but usually given information along the lines of 'what the chart says', and there the matter ends. For a growing number of people this has been something of a gulf—a 'set-adrift' point at which the client is equipped with a great deal of astrological information (which may, in fact, be worth knowing) that remains unfocused upon the actual circumstances he is experiencing. As mentioned earlier, people do not want to be merely interpreted, classified and disassembled for analysis like bits of a machine; there is an individual behind every birth chart who wants to be understood and reach new realizations and awarenesses. Particularly if an insightful translation of the birth chart is being rendered, what is more natural than to want to talk with someone who seems to know you so well? It is like finding a socket into which one may at last plug some loose wires.

Thus, if one important turning point in ensuring a better relationship towards astrology has lain in a willingness to let go of it as an oracle of external fate and fortune, another has hinged upon our willingness to move beyond one-sided and rigid interpretations, which have the nature only of inflexible character studies.

2.
THE UNIVERSE AND THE INDIVIDUAL

Astrology used within a counselling framework sees the individual and the universe as interrelated and interdependent—each existing within and reflecting the other in a two-way dance. The birth chart provides a frame of reference by which a person can become more aware of this reciprocal relationship and thus participate more consciously in it.

Much difficulty exists (both in and out of the astrological world) in knowing just how astrology works and much research is continuing by scientists, biologists, astrologers and others in order to find both material causes and meaningful explanations for the interconnections between celestial and terrestrial phenomena. On the one hand there are enquiries along deterministic lines of planetary effects, but at the same time we also live in a world where our attention is called to that which lies outside causality, where we perceive the cycles of our existence and celestial patterns as a mutual reflection, each simultaneously resonating the other. Our language rarely lends itself to a description of this interrelationship, which is satisfying to the logical mind because it calls for a different line of understanding from objective inference. While we live on a physical planet and can look upwards, our perceptions of the outer reality (those other physical planets in the heavens) are not divorced from our inner experience. From this framework, the universe is regarded as one Whole, one totality, and this places the individual on earth in a position of essential unity with that which surrounds him, rather than one in which he is an isolated unit living on a planet whirling somewhere in space. The human being takes part in the universe as well as observing it and parallels to this fundamental unity of all things have been reflected in the concepts of modern physicists since the turn of the century. To pursue these lines of thought further, the reader is particularly referred to *The Tao of Physics* by Fritjof Capra and also to C. G. Jung's discussion of his concept of synchronicity in his Foreword to the *I Ching or Book of Changes* (Richard Wilhelm translation).

To the astrological counsellor, the chart of a person's birth is both astronomically a map of the solar system at a given moment and astrologically a fundamental guide to the pattern of viable energies, drives, capacities and capabilities within the person born at that moment. In this respect, a good and frequently used analogy is of a seed packet bearing a picture of the plant or flower those seeds are intended to become. By working with his birth chart, the individual can trace and become acquainted with the nature of the basic processes and drives (the seeds) he manifests in his life as general or specific experiences as he develops (plant or flower). By further analogy, he can conceive of his life more as a tapestry of interwoven colours, textures and patterns, with himself as the central weaver, not as a purposeless chaotic jumble which he just has to get through somehow.

As the quotation from Rudhyar at the beginning of this book points out, the moment the astrologer puts the client in touch with his chart she introduces him to a *relationship* . . . a relationship of unity with his cosmos. Since he has a part in it too, he can shift his astrological conversations from 'What is Saturn going to do to me when it transits my Sun?' to 'How can I use this instruction in the heavens and put it into practice, apply it for my life and the way it is developing?' 'What does this transit mean for me?' can reciprocally become 'and what do I mean for it?' The 'instruction' just mentioned is not understood as a precise and clearly-defined event. The heavens do not say that in March you are going to have a depressing time in your love life because Saturn will transit your Venus in the seventh house. What it says is that the process for you, the individual, to bring to life is a concrete scrutiny (Saturn) of your inner values (Venus) concerning interpersonal relationships (seventh house). The individual may well focus the main theme of this process upon a key relationship in his life; the manifestation might be ending a relationship, putting an existing relationship on to a different footing, starting a relationship—in fact anything that will reflect the requirement made of the individual to focus upon personal boundaries, feelings, needs, fears, direction and truths when relating to another person. The astrological counsellor cannot impose upon the individual what it will be, but is in a position to help him find the significance of whatever experience he goes through by putting him in touch with the theme and process behind it.

3.
THE NATURE OF ASTROLOGICAL COUNSELLING

So far, we have seen that the modern frame of reference within which today's astrological counsellor works is of the zodiacal signs and planets as *representations* of the basic energies, needs, drives, and qualities contained within man and reciprocally projected by him upon the heavens. These inner processes—for example, the capacity to love (Venus and Mars), for assertion (Mars), perception (Mercury, Uranus), for social involvement (the last six zodiacal signs), the development of resources (second house, Taurus), and so on—are common to all human beings, but the particular pattern or arrangement of them at the moment of the individual's birth renders him unique.

It is by the joint discovery of the interplay of these processes in the individual chart pattern, by the astrologer and client working *together* as a team, that the particular way the client manifests them in his life (via character expression, behaviour, events, etc.) can achieve greater clarity. For example, a Mercury/Saturn conjunction represents the union of two processes: the individual's capacity for perception, awareness, thought and the communication of ideas (Mercury) with his sense of structure, form, practicality, boundaries and restrictions (Saturn). In turn, those processes merge into general themes in the person's life via efficiency, practicality and method in mental pursuits (such as the ability for concentrated study, careful scrutiny of ideas, concrete and specific ways of communicating), or alternatively the experience of limit, control, obstacles and restrictions on his views, ideas, speech (perhaps feeling frightened to express an opinion or voice his ideas, getting bogged down in thought, or difficulty in learning or studying). The actual end-manifestation may lie within any of these basic principles and themes and on many different levels. It can only become clear when the astrologer and client meet to work together on the chart.

Having explained the intrinsic nature of the chart factor to the client, the astrologer can help him relate it to his life as he knows it: How does he recognize this process in his life? How has he used it so far? What are his past experiences and environment and have they lent colour and direction to the way he expresses it now? Has he developed it at all, or does it seem to be a factor in his chart which, in life, is lying dormant? By her experience of the client in their session together, the astrologer can often help him into seeing how he uses these planetary energies. She may make suggestions as to their usual manifestations in human beings and apply them both to what she knows of his life and to how she sees them being expressed in their work together. More particularly, through conversation with the client she will guide him into his own individual lines of discovery. We shall see something of this particular planetary aspect (Mercury/Saturn) in the example of Robert on page 87.

Stated briefly, it is this shared participation between astrologer and client that constitutes the kernel of astrological counselling. It marks the third important shift in perspective mentioned in the first chapter, since it places the client in a position of self-determination in his life and not one of helplessness or powerlessness in relation to set interpretations insisted upon by the astrologer. It also opens the client to making more aware choices from which to create his future.

The concepts and insights of modern psychology (particularly the depth psychology of C. G. Jung) are particularly helpful to the astrological counsellor, for, although psychological philosophies and the learning of theories do not of themselves necessarily make for an effective counselling relationship between astrologer and client, nevertheless their importance lies principally in the fact that they do compel us to recognize that a human being is not a static model suitable for fixed interpretations and superficial judgements but (like the universe) is a dynamic and complex living system in which everything is in constant flow, ever changing. Particularly since the early 1960s, we have witnessed a remarkable escalation of man's need to get to know himself better and recognize his many facets, via widespread revitalization of psychological and spiritual education—depth psychologies, the newer therapies of the 'growth movement', Eastern philosophies, esoteric teachings, alternative approaches to physical health, parapsychological studies and so on. Even those who have no active interest in astrology are aware that we are at the interface of what is called 'The Age of Aquarius'—so much so, that the phrase (or its derivatives, such as 'New Age') have become part of our language. The astrological ages are related to the movement out of alignment between the wheel of the zodiacal signs and the wheel of the constellations (groups of stars), both of which have the same names. This movement is known as the precession of the equinoxes and, briefly, means that each year, because of the Earth's rotation on a tilted axis, the first degree of the sign Aries (the vernal equinox) moves very very slightly backwards. So, although at one time the zodiacal sign Aries and the constellation of Aries were once matched in alignment, over thousands of years the movement has been such that they are no longer so. In fact, it takes about 26,000 years for a complete cycle to be made and for the last 2,000 years, 0° Aries has been moving against the background of the constellation of Pisces. It is now reaching the last stars of that constellation and moving into the first stars of the constellation of Aquarius. At the dawning of each New Age in history the collective values of mankind are in deep transition, with outpourings of developments, attitudes, and events in the world that describe the nature of that transition.

From the point of view of astrological counselling, this current New Age upsurge has brought very many people to the awareness that our lives are not merely a series of outer events—being born, going to school, taking examinations, getting a job, marriage, children, retirement, death—but that all of the steps we take are points along a particular pathway, which each of us refers to as 'my life'. All of them not only describe our outer development from child to old person, but also bear witness to our inner development. Here, too, depth psychology has helped put astrological understandings into perspective. Many people try to live cocooned only in what they consciously know of themselves. But, beneath this, there is a much larger reservoir containing many other levels to which all of our actions, ideas, decisions, feelings, motives are also subject—what depth psychology calls 'the unconscious'. The recognition of these other levels puts us in touch with meaning in our lives; it opens us up to the reality of our spiritual as well as animal nature; it puts us in touch with everything we experience and helps us to make sense of it all. Astrologically, this discovery lies in understanding the whole celestial pattern: planets, signs, aspects, houses, angles, progressions, cycles, and so on.

It was the musician-philosopher-astrologer, Dane Rudhyar, who largely initiated an integration of psychological, spiritual and astrological insights as far back as the mid-1930s, an integration that was fostered by many others around that time and has been since. It leads us essentially to an astrology through which we can grow, as opposed to one which keeps us where we are, held within the confines of fixed character interpretations. In many ways, this kind of astrology, which seeks to promote the growth and development of the individual is still, in practice, in something of an embryonic state and, like any embryo, needs nurturing as it grows. It also takes time, for shifts in perception made by human beings, including astrologers, are accompanied by many initial struggles as they free themselves from older concepts and reach for new understandings.

Rudhyar has said that events do not happen to us but that we happen to them and, today, subsidiary questions such as 'How am I contributing to this situation? What am I learning/achieving/ understanding/completing/initiating by having this event in my life? Where am I taking myself through living this current crisis?' all form the core of the day-to-day issues of loving, working, aloneness, joy, hopes, failure and the other multitudinous experiences that make up our lives. These issues in turn are all brought to the astrological counsellor's attention, as, of course, they are to that of others in similar situations and professions.

All such people, whether they are counsellors, analysts, therapists, or social workers, have potential value for the person in difficulty or need. Each has a different framework from the other and different experiences, personal realities, abilities, beliefs and attitudes, and it is important for them, as it is for anyone who puts themselves in the position of a helper, to work on their *own* self-awareness as well as concerning themselves with that of other people.

Bearing this in mind, what is so helpful in astrology is that the frame of reference the counsellor uses (i.e. the birth chart) is intrinsically that of the client also and through an understanding of the chart, the recognition by the astrologer of the client's innate disposition and potential is more immediate than that of others in similar fields, who may work with the person for weeks, or even months, before the essential points of the client's nature become clear. Even so, astrological counsellors are aware that other kinds of counsellors and other therapeutic approaches have key values for the client also and are ready to open up their work to include these, by personal participation, by training if possible, and by the referral of their clients to appropriate help elsewhere.

4.
THE BIRTH CHART AS A GUIDE IN OUR DEVELOPMENT

If the birth chart is seen as a pattern of energies within the individual, who comes into the world at the moment the entire cosmos resonates their essential nature, it seems clear that there is much to be discovered at personal, gradual and subliminal levels in order for him to relate to the pattern as a whole and grasp its significances in his life. The planetary positions and aspects within the signs and houses represent symbolically all that goes to make up the rhythm of the person, his nature and his life. An initial interpretation of the birth chart provides a reference point and the shared counselling work stepping-stones to the much wider voyage of self-discovery that is continually in process for all of us. Not everyone wants to make these conscious steps, of course, and for some it may be unsuitable to do so; but, additionally, very often when we talk in terms of 'inner development' and 'symbols' in everyday life, we can run into difficulties straight away, for such phrases can be the object of scorn or ridicule, or at least mild amusement.

It all sounds rather abstruse and philosophical and some find it infinitely preferable to live life responding only to the demands of their outer life—more money, a better job, a more exciting relationship—unaware of their inner personal influence upon the determination of that outside world. At times of deep anxiety, when we feel there is no meaning, no sense of joy, fullness or richness in life, or when there is an increasing sense of futility, of goals forever unattainable, or when we feel without the resources to cope, we may *touch* upon some inner questioning along the lines of 'What am I here for? What is the purpose of my life?' But in a busy and rushing world we may just as frequently drive ourselves into finding or creating some kind of 'certitude' (like the new job or a change of environment), or we throw more parties, or change our diet, or buy ourselves some new clothes—anything that we feel might change all the negative feelings and give us a sense of purpose, direction, a fresh start. But it often turns out that although we may have a different backdrop, we are in fact crying the same tears, meeting the same problems in other guises.

We cannot avoid problems, crises and suffering; indeed they are necessary to our development. People (indeed sometimes whole nations) intermittently pass through difficult points of experience in order to know themselves more fully. It is a question of becoming aware that within each of us there is a very deep source—or core, centre—which, while living our practical day-to-day life, is at the nub of all that we encounter, both outwardly and inwardly. A symbol, such as a particular planet symbolizing a particular need or drive within us, serves to suggest an underlying meaning, not to indicate an exact and mechanical, or logical, connection. The astrological chart helps us to understand what makes up our experience and development by aligning us to the central life processes within us all that guide us on and beckon us forward.

The Jungian analyst June Singer describes astrology in relation to the exploration of the psyche (the totality of all that is conscious and unconscious within us) as 'a map, a pattern, a model, that helps us understand our place in the entire scheme of things'.[*] This is a useful analogy to follow for it is by using the birth chart as an initial 'route-finder' that the astrological counsellor, faced with someone who has a worry, a problem or a crisis in hand, or who is perhaps simply feeling aimless, confused or in some kind of vacuum, can help that person alter his perception and orientation from 'this is happening to me' (conceiving of himself merely at the receiving-end of whatever happens to happen). Instead, they can explore together the 'ingredients' contained within the particular situation and the client can be helped to see it in the context of his life as a whole. To do this, the astrologer will explain by translating the fundamental human processes they represent within him and

[*] June Singer, *Androgyny—Towards a New Theory of Sexuality*.

which have constellated the situation he is experiencing. Indeed, these are the only factors about the situation that could be said to be 'fated'. We cannot, for example, halt Uranus en route to its transit of, say, our natal Sun position; we can, however, choose *how* we live out the process of transformation and change (Uranus) by understanding the implications of this experience in relation to the development of our life at a particular time. Therefore, the actual way in which we imprint ourselves upon the transit is a matter of free will.

Having adjusted to the basic perspectives we need to follow to construct a modern frame of reference for the practice of astrological counselling, we can now look at the contents of the birth chart itself and how they emerge through the medium of people talking. In Part III first steps in consulting an astrological counsellor will be covered, as well as some main issues that can arise for consideration by astrologer and client alike.

PART 2:
THE BIRTH CHART

5.
THE PLANETS AND ANGLES IN COUNSELLING

The planets within our solar system represent basic life impulses in every human being—impulses that stimulate and motivate us into different forms of expressing ourselves, both in our activity and in our being. The Sun and Moon are not properly planets, although for convenience they are generally referred to as such. The Sun is usually the only factor that people probably know something about astrologically, since they know the zodiac sign it occupied at the time they were born. However, when a full birth chart is drawn up, the newcomer to astrology first becomes aware that his nature and make-up is not only symbolized in his being born 'a Gemini' or 'a Capricorn', or any one particular sign, but that he—like every other individual—is born with all ten planets (including the Sun and Moon) in his celestial map and surrounded by all twelve zodiacal signs.

THE SUN AND MOON
The Sun, as we know, is the centre of our solar system and is the source of all that is life-giving and life-sustaining. Astrologically, it is similarly considered as a symbol of all that goes to make up our

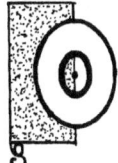

vitality, our drive, our will and spur toward integration. This is not easy, and indeed is ultimately what the whole life is about; for what we are seeking to integrate through the essential heart of the Sun's position in our birth charts (and by extension the inmost purpose of our existence) is everything else that appears in the chart—all those other planets, signs, aspects (every other impulse and drive within the individual) which flow to and through that centre in the person represented by the Sun in his chart.

So the position of Sun in the person's chart defines his essential purpose and is also subject to all other levels of his nature and experience. Through the Sun's position by sign, house, aspects, the astrological counsellor can guide the client into knowing more clearly the central identity which he *needs must* cultivate and express. It is not at all a question of saying 'You're a Scorpio, therefore you're powerful and intense and can be very jealous', but more a question of aligning the client to the crucial necessity of fulfilling the essential process of Scorpio. Sometimes a person may function only minimally from the Sun's position in the chart, particularly if he is young, but he will usually develop more of its essence as he gets older and becomes aware of and redefines or adjusts other levels of his whole being. Sometimes a person may be so out of touch with the needs of his Sun, that life for him can become rather like trying to keep a car going when there is no petrol in the tank, or no oil in the engine. He 'fizzles out' into some kind of deterioration, the wear and tear being signalled by psychological or physical disorientation (or both)—upset, exhaustion, dissipation, the havoc wreaked diminishing in proportion to the amount of Sun he then allows to shine through again in his life.

Because the sign containing the Sun has become popularly known for certain sets of characteristics, some people feel that they are either 'good', or nice, or 'bad', not nice—Scorpio, Virgo and Capricorn notoriously faring less well in the popularity stakes than other signs! Consequently, many people mistakenly feel that they must stop a person with the Sun in what they regard as a 'not nice' sign from being that character. But the Sun represents more of a *purpose* than outward and set characteristics and in astrological counselling the importance lies not in calling a halt to the client's expression of his Sun sign, but of unveiling its first principles, its inner processes, so that the client can use these as a stepping-stone to *being* and *living* his Sun in a fulfilling way for his life as a whole.

Alongside the Sun, **the Moon's** position in the birth chart provides a counter-balance to the active principle of purpose signified by the Sun. It symbolizes a complementary, passive and responsive feeling reaction within the individual. As the satellite of the Earth, the

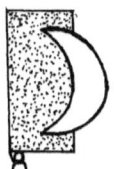 Moon's position in relation to us is that of an intimate companion and in relation to the central Sun it is a reflector of light. Symbolically, therefore, the astrological principle of the Moon is one of softer illumination and represents that which is close, instinctively hugged to us, our deep-rooted and habitual feelings, which (like the ocean's tides, also responding to the rhythms of the Moon) ebb and flow through our moods, inconstancies, vagaries of emotional reaction, our receptivity to experience, the way we absorb changing patterns, our sensory responses—all of which emerge through different phases of experience, just as we on the Earth see the Moon passing through its phases, the cycle from one New Moon to another.

The way in which we develop the quality of our Moon level stems very much from our early familial and inherited conditionings— our origins, the past and the instinctive relating patterns derived from these, particularly in our immediate family environment and more particularly from the mother. Indeed, the function of the Moon is most clearly exhibited by a baby, who simply responds to the only universe he knows, which is his coexistence with his mother, with all of its varying patterns of warmth, light, hunger, sleeping, waking, etc. Thus it represents a response pattern automatically followed without prior intent or design and underlies repetitive habit-patterns, which predominate in our feelings, thoughts and actions. Quite often in astrological counselling, when a client reports his particular response to a situation and adds the words 'Do you know, this is *always* the case with me', the corresponding area of the chart reflecting the experience can highlight the Moon's position and strength in the chart.

Whether positively or negatively expressed, the essence of the Moon is familiar and habitual to the person concerned, therefore 'safe'. Thus, another way we can connect to the meaning of the Moon in our charts is to consider it in terms of the haven we constantly run back to when the going gets tough in life and we are under stress. It is often discernible by the astrological counsellor working with a client who is undergoing such a period of stress. It is also a 'return point' for us when we are not particularly doing or being anything, but simply relaxing, absorbing. In short, the condition of the Moon in a person's chart will give insight and guidance to the counsellor on the manner in which a person most expeditiously maintains his inner sense of emotional and physical well-being in terms of what is familiar and instinctive to him, whilst striving to fulfil the energies signified by the Sun in his chart.

These two energies of Sun and Moon will be co-ordinated by the astrological counsellor when considering the birth chart and guiding her client to understand its relevance and potential unfoldment. Although we shall be looking at the signs more closely in a later section, for the moment we may say, by way of example, that a person with the Sun in Aries and Moon in Capricorn could be said to be someone whose central purpose for development is that of an initiator, one who needs to use propulsive energy in order to create new enterprises and meet challenges (Aries). His instinctive needs revolve around the criteria of certitude, structure, constancy, conformity (Capricorn).

Thus a Sun/Moon blend of assertion and prudent caution will form a key theme in this person's life and it is the job of the astrological counsellor to explore with the client the way in which this theme is lived out by him and the possibilities for its future development, particularly if it constitutes a conflict—which might well be the case in this particular example where the Sun's energies through Aries lend themselves to a 'get-up-and-go-devil-may-care' attitude, while deep down the lunar instincts may be more for 'let's-stay-put-awhile-till-I'm-more-sure-of-my-ground'! Alternatively, a combination of the Sun and Moon blend in these two signs could be developed as a very dynamic ambition coupled with controlled power—the person displaying much enterprise and tough determination to assert himself and stand his ground.

THE FOUR ANGLES: Ascendant/Descendant: MC/IC

These two axes of horizon and meridian respectively mark the orientation of the individual in his encounter with the outer world, both in terms of how he expresses himself to it (Ascendant/Descendant) and the foundation from which he directs his aims and priorities (IC/MC). The angles can only be calculated when the time and location of birth are known as well as the date, thus marking the individual's point of entry to the world—his moment of birth.

The Ascendant/Descendant Axis: The Ascendant reflects the way the individual prefers to approach life and other people. The sign on the Ascendant (often called the Rising Sign) describes the impress he makes and which others will see when they meet him. It

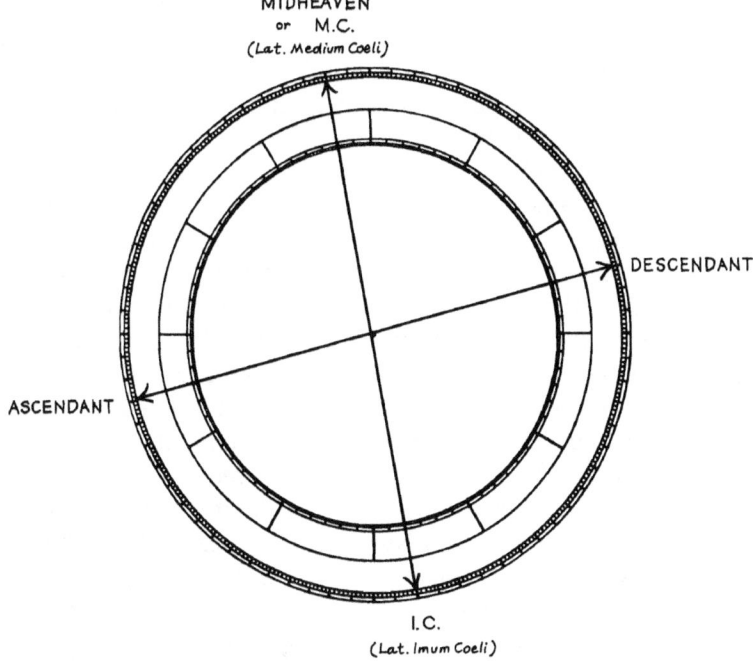

Figure 1. The Four Angles.

can often be very different from what is going on inside the individual at the Sun and Moon and other levels, but it denotes the threshold the person steps into and over in order to relate to what is outside of him. It is a vantage point from which he surveys the world through the 'camera lens' of his own beliefs and needs and through which he expresses other levels of the chart.

To one person the outside world may be one which he needs to meet by being challenging and assertive (and he may have Aries rising); for another it may be with curiosity and restlessness (Gemini); for another, with intensity and persistence (Scorpio), and so on. Another way of looking at the Ascendant area of the birth chart is that although none of us spontaneously remembers our birth moment, there is considerable agreement among psychologists who have conducted research into birth experience that many 'decisions' are made concerning the nature of the world by the individual entering it, according to *its* impact upon *him* and *his* impact upon *it* as he emerges from the womb into independent life. Whatever the essence of this impact, it colours and permeates the person's subsequent approach to life and, astrologically, may be mirrored by the Ascendant. Although there is insufficient astrological experience and data to propose this as an immutable fact, nevertheless a number of people who have experienced 'rebirthing' as part of their own psychotherapeutic process report the experience in ways which 'speak' their Ascendants, and this would perhaps provide an interesting project for further research.

The Ascendant does not *cause* this quality of approach and impact within us, but if we consider that our nature puts us where and when we need to be, then this point in the chart (which is necessarily dependent for its calculation upon time and location) most resonates our need for self-expression and self-projection. In astrological counselling, the sign on the Ascendant, together with any planets around it, will guide us to the premiss from which the client perceives and experiences his world, which in turn dictates how he meets it. The Ascendant can also be experienced by both client and counsellor in one another when they meet, the point of embarkation on their work together being coloured personally by each of them in terms of their respective rising signs.

Whereas the Ascendant reflects the individual's approach and stamp on his environment, its opposite point, **the Descendant**, reflects his participation in the world as a social being; it is where he becomes aware of the significance of other people through his experience of them. It marks an exchange of energy between himself and others and particularly reflects the quality of his one-to-one relationships, such as marriage. A person may come to the astrological counsellor with a relationship/marital difficulty and much of the way in which he describes his partner will portray the qualities of his own Descendant. This is *his* chart and therefore these qualities are those that he *would be*, complementary to those that he *is* being at the Ascendant. Thus, they need to be met via a partner (or indeed an enemy) so that he can know them in himself; the significance and experience of them then renders him more complete. It can be thought of as the other-half to the Ascendant which, when incorporated, takes the individual to a fulfilment of this whole axis. For a particularly lucid exposition of this axis from the point of view of relationships, the reader is referred to a chapter entitled 'The Inner Partner' in the book *Relating—An Astrological Guide to Living with Others on a Small Planet* by Liz Greene (see Appendix I). However, this Descendant point is not only concerned with our emotional relationships; it also has to do with any situation/relationship in which we are required to negotiate, befriend and include 'the other' as an extension, albeit unconscious, of ourselves.

The MC/IC Axis: This axis represents the individual's concrete striving in the world (MC) and the foundations upon which these endeavours are based (IC)—or, what one stands for and the 'legs' on which one stands. The MC reflects the individual's operation in the world and the type of qualities and experiences he most needs to adhere to in order to fulfill his goals. It is the way he wants the world at large to see him, the criteria to which he most aspires, that which he holds in most esteem, seeks to develop in himself and be acknowledged for. Both points of this axis can be difficult for the person to relate to, but particularly **the IC** which represents a most unknown part of ourselves. It symbolizes a deeply subjective level of our being which, although obscure, nevertheless gives significance to the realization of our goals at the MC. The IC can be thought of as a sort of withdrawal point, to which analogies and images may provide a better guide than words, and various astrological writers have used apt ones, such as a tree (the roots, IC; the branches at the top, MC; the whole axis, the trunk); also a ladder (bottom rungs IC, top rungs MC, the whole axis symbolizing the climb). Thus the MC can be thought of as the individual's personal 'excelsior', the IC opposite his point of recoil, where he is rooted, where he periodically touches base, then to return back into the world and his endeavours. It can likewise be regarded as a private person—public person axis. The MC is easier for us to relate to in our minds since it refers to that which we reach for on a conscious level (public person); the IC is a more veiled area, denoting that within us which underpins those aims (the private person).

In astrological counselling, this axis is looked at as the backbone or mainstay by which the person develops criteria and pursues objectives. Quite often, therefore, the signs and planets surrounding both points of the axis may be reflected in a particular career and in the personal 'launch-pad' from which this career is pursued. The axis can also reflect the people the client relates to, inasmuch as they cater to and uphold the values symbolized by both points. In turn, these criteria are partly built upon the life-experience of parental or inherited values, because the way we strive for anything in the outer world is collected up via the norms we internalize in our upbringing and development. Accumulated 'signals' from early environmental authority figures (such as mother and father) point us up to something we most feel we can dedicate ourselves to, set our sights upon. The two points of MC and IC (together mainly with Sun, Moon and Saturn in the chart) also reflect the roles and characters we ascribe to our parents in the process of our growth through childhood, together with the values which we deem they hold. Very often we may follow careers or other goals in life which our parents also followed or which were otherwise, in essence, held in esteem by them. In astrological counselling, the discussion of this axis can arise in situations where the person is endeavouring to separate out how much of it he is developing for himself and how much may be being lived out (and perhaps continued for) one or other or both of his parents. It is frequently at a time of planetary progressions or transits over this axis (and indeed the Ascendant/Descendant) that their meanings come to attention to be understood, long transits of outer planets being of particular significance—as in the case of Natasha, whom we shall meet in Part III.

PERSONAL PLANETS: Mercury: Venus: Mars

Although astrologers have gathered traditional set meanings for planets through collected information and observations over the centuries, the astrological counsellor concentrates first on their basic principles, which can have a wide variety of 'meanings' when brought to life by a human being with all of his changes, complexities and transitions. One way in which we can understand the life-principles of planets is by referring to their position in the solar system in relation to the Earth (*Figure 2.*). Both Mercury and Venus lie between the Earth and the central Sun and their meaning as extended into our lives concerns that which is of an inward nature. Mars, as the first planet out from the Earth, is appropriately invested with that which is externalized after being grounded and given form (on the Earth). Additionally, the sequence of planetary paths around the Sun flows through two wavelengths, rather like the ebb and flow of blood from and back to the heart via the arteries and veins in the human body.

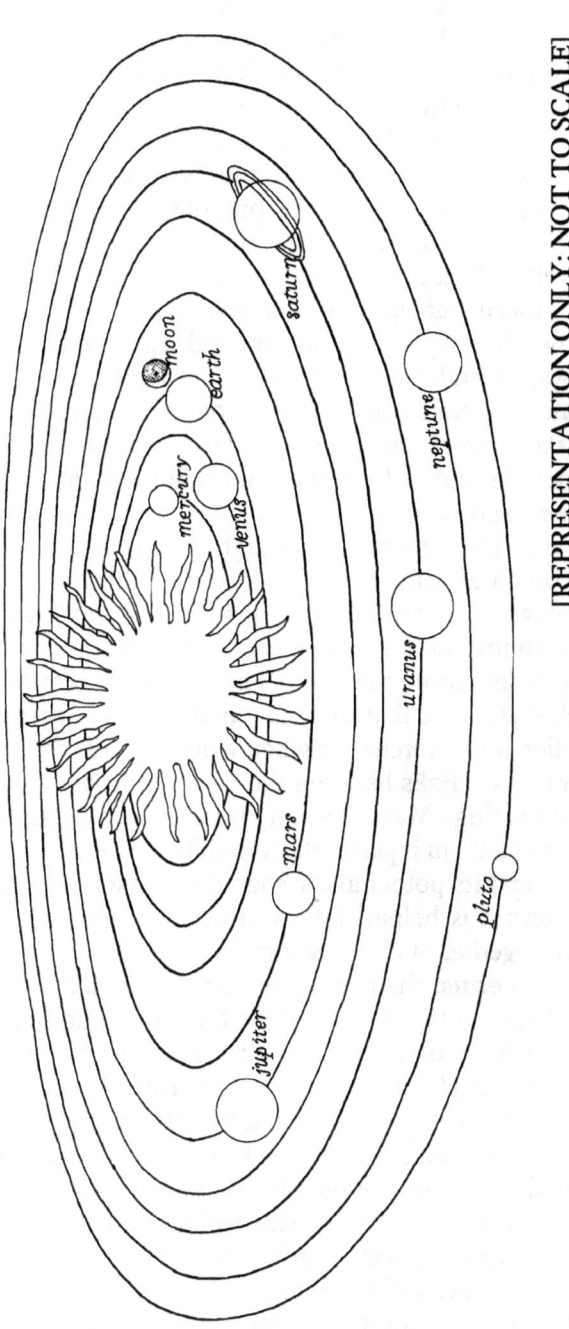

[REPRESENTATION ONLY: NOT TO SCALE]

Figure 2. The Solar System.

Mercury, positioned closest to the Sun, stands rather as one who introduces the solar energy to all the other planets, and vice-versa. Thus, his function is that of an introductory link, transmission, connection and we may liken Mercury to a go-between, an agent or a courier between the Sun and the rest of the solar system. On an incoming wavelength, this function is experienced within the individual as recognition, perception and awareness. On an outgoing wavelength, it is that which spurs us toward the communication of those perceptions and awarenesses. In astrological counselling, Mercury's sign, element and aspects will guide us to a person's way of understanding (which does not always first occur through mental constructs), the way that he is most able to 'plug in' and make sense of what is explained to him from the birth chart, the channel through which the counsellor can most help him connect with and become consciously aware of that which he is experiencing. This might be through using clear language, or through practical suggestions, through drawing analogies, through images, fantasies, feelings. It will also point the way to the lines of communication the client uses in his participation with the counsellor in discussing the chart. The counsellor's own Mercury can be looked at also so that she is in touch with her own propensity for perception and interchange when working with her client. She can also watch for links between the two charts, her own and her client's, involving Mercury—for instance, a Moon/Mercury contact between them is particularly helpful for the purpose of their relationship and its potential for shared understanding; a Saturn/Mercury contact is helpful for constructive clarification in their exploration together of chart factors.

Venus, the next planet out from Mercury, also lies between the Earth and the Sun, standing rather in the position of one who joins in and co-operates with Mercury's initial connecting role. Venus continues bringing the vitality of the Sun closer to us, refining the recognition/perception of Mercury by giving them meaning and value. In the human individual Venus symbolizes that which we care about, appreciate, feel ready to unite with in co-operation and alliance. Venus in the birth chart guides us to the mainspring of the person's likes and dislikes, his needs for concord and rapport through closeness, love, sharing, and beauty. On an

outgoing wavelength, the process of Venus is carried through the individual's affections, his urge to attract and unite with others, to beautify his world and to love, and also what he needs to value in himself in order to feel loved.

In astrological counselling, this planet's position in the chart helps us to understand the way a person enters into, and lives out, what is pleasurable to him, what aligns him most clearly to his true inner values, even though these may not always be shared by others around him. In relationships, it reflects the way he will feel most appreciated and, reciprocally, the way he feels he can best bestow affection upon another. His drive towards sharing generally can also be considered, and Venus will reflect what he personally likes in terms of what is beautiful, pleasing, worthwhile, or what simply makes him feel good. As such, it also underlies the accumulation of anything which, to him, is of value, desirable or aesthetically pleasing, whether tangible or not—a bouquet of flowers, a walk in the country, a valuable painting, quiet contemplation; but not only that which is delicate for some people's tastes and desires may be of a more raucous nature than is traditionally associated with Venus.

Sometimes the counsellor can help the client mobilize the drive towards well-being signified by Venus when he is feeling 'low', but only if and when it is appropriate to the client. In other words, without negating or sweeping aside the client's unhappy feelings, the counsellor may, at certain stages of the work together, be able to guide him into focusing on ways to 'connect' within to what he finds most uplifting, ways to give back to himself the feeling of being a person of worth, appreciated and accepted. In this sense, we can reflect upon Venus as an indicator of our inner resources and our potential for self-help in order to restore us to a sense of equilibrium at times of stress and difficulty. Focusing upon inner values can also very often be a feature for the client whose Venus receives aspects from, say, Neptune or Saturn. In the former case, he may be living out a situation in which they are being sacrificed up to something or someone else; in the latter he may not feel that he is allowed to express his true needs, nor valued. It is also important for the counsellor to be aware of her own Venus when working with clients, since periodically she may need to ensure that her part of the work is catering to the client's needs and not merely to what constitutes her own comfort and ease. For example, the counsellor may have Venus in Gemini and what makes her feel good is to talk and talk, have several people around her, or be constantly busy; her client, on the other hand, may have Venus in Pisces and may well feel better if he is allowed to be tranquil; he may perhaps even want to cry, and thus feel more deeply into an experience as a way of evaluating its meaning. Similarly, aspects between the client's Venus and the counsellor's chart can be looked at to assess the potential ease or difficulty, helpfulness or otherwise, of their work together, which is, after all, an alliance.

Mars is the first planet out from the Earth and thus symbolizes where we start to move outward from the physical form (Earth) and have decisive impact. Its process is one of initiating drive; it is the way we take action and assert ourselves. Building up on our previous impulses of recognition and evaluation (Mercury and Venus), we release them through our physical, emotional and intellectual strengths. Mars in a person's birth chart will guide us to his quality of enterprise, the type of power and endurance he expresses. Some people only equate this planet with warlike qualities—a bellowing, raging, aggressive energy, and in some signs it may well be experienced via that type of high level 'push'. However, in the main we may regard the process of Mars in astrological counselling as being indicative of the kind of energy a person needs to use to precipitate any kind of outward occurrence —the action needed to deal with a problem, create a situation, start a relationship, etc. It is the way the person is most able to go about things, to proclaim and put into action what (with Venus) he holds most desirable.

As such, it can also reflect the kind of energy he puts into his work with the counsellor. A person with Mars in Taurus may exhibit a steady and persistent energy in the counselling work, chewing matters over carefully and taking each step resolutely; whereas Mars in Gemini may exhibit a great deal of restless energy, perhaps wanting to dart about from one part of the chart to another very quickly, or asking a lot of questions. Similarly, the counsellor's own chart position of Mars will reflect the way she goes about her work and aspects between their two charts involving Mars will point the counsellor and client to areas where their energies will blend, or be a potential source of irritation. Positive aspects between them can be developed in getting to grips actively with the work in hand, while aspects that emerge negatively may need careful handling if the respective energies of both people are not to degenerate into a clashing battle for control.

JUPITER AND SATURN
Having started to move outwards from the Earth, meeting Mars and taking definite action to assert ourselves, we then move further afield in the solar system, into a vast area that takes us through the rocky belt of the asteroids, then on further, until we come to Jupiter, the largest planet in the whole system. Beyond this lies Saturn, uniquely encircled by delicate rings in the plane of its equator and which at one time was thought to be the last planet in the system.

Thus, in meeting these two planets, we have (a) moved further out into space and (b) come across a boundary—and symbolically these become the processes of Jupiter and Saturn within the human being. **Jupiter** symbolizes for us where we seek to broaden and expand our experience in ways which will take us onward to fulfilment. Our well-being through Jupiter comes via experiencing a step out into something more spacious, more abundant in our lives—something which gives us more breadth, more scope, and augments what we experienced before. Therefore, in the birth chart it represents where one seeks an expansion in growth, to feel 'greater than' (reflecting Jupiter being greater in mass than all the planets together). We can develop confidence with Jupiter, and its position on the birth chart will help us understand what gives the person most meaning, most fulfilment, most faith in himself; it will also give an idea of those areas of life in which he can be prolific, fruitful, and where he can grow, if he makes the journey outward to reach it. With Jupiter we open a door on to something that gives us more latitude.

Quite often, people come to the astrological counsellor at times when this particular area of the chart is being brought into focus (by progression or transit) and the ensuing discussion can help the client into deciding what has most meaning and fulfilment for him. For example, a client may have Jupiter in Cancer in the seventh house and be experiencing a period of inner questioning, concerning the pursuit of fulfilment in establishing relationships he cares about, within which he can develop his nurturing and concern for others. Perhaps he wants to get married and have children; perhaps he wants to open up a centre for homeless people; perhaps he wants to embark on a business partnership in a chain of restaurants. In whatever way the essence of Cancer and the seventh house are being manifested by him, Jupiter's position here will point the counsellor towards the client's sense of meaning, belief, faith and fulfilment—whatever constitutes his personal 'cornucopia'.

But we cannot follow Jupiter's path *ad infinitum*, for its theme of abundance can become magnified into over-inflation, exaggeration and aggrandizement unless we place a limit upon it. There is only a certain extent to which we can stretch a rubber band until it rebounds upon us, or snaps, and **Saturn** stands beyond Jupiter in the solar system to remind us of that. Before Uranus was discovered in 1781, Saturn was thought to be the outermost planet—the end of the sequence, the boundary, the limit. Symbolically, its correlative function in the human being amounted to just that— restriction, restraint, a finality, a closure, termination, extremity. In contrast to Jupiter's expansion, Saturn became contraction and for a long time has been regarded negatively and often in dire terms— the bitter end, oppression, harshness, severity, austerity—a true 'bogeyman' of the solar system! A friend of mine tells me that in America one can buy something called a 'cuddly Saturn' (a soft toy), which I suppose is one way of befriending this planet and imbuing it with love!

We do most decidedly need to understand and care about Saturn's position on our birth charts, for although no one likes restriction and oppression in their lives, we frequently enter periods in which we need to look at areas of our being (which perhaps we do not really want to!) in order to get a fuller understanding of how we may be creating, inviting or contributing to such negativities. This often means that we go through testing situations where there are 'lessons' to be learned and where we encounter some of our deep-rooted fears. The astrological counsellor will therefore give extremely careful consideration to the position of Saturn on the birth chart, for this guides her to where the person feels most vulnerable or inferior, weak or insecure.

These feelings of inadequacy lead us to put up defences against them and therefore Saturn can also show us the sort of wall we build up to avoid facing in ourselves particular weaknesses and inner pain. Today, and from the point of view of where we are in our psychological education, we understand a great deal about how we defend ourselves against these 'dark' areas inside us; we know, for instance, that while we may maintain these defences for a while we cannot go on trying to keep our inner weaknesses hidden in the hope that they will go away—apart from anything else they have a nasty habit of escaping when we least expect it! We also know that we cannot present ourselves to the world only as some kind of perfect person with no weaknesses at all, and so we are left with the prospect of facing and dealing with them. Of course it can be painful to face the less pleasant aspects of our nature, but it is not nearly as burdensome as trying to keep them out of sight.

The symbolic representation of a boundary that Saturn affords us shows us where 'the buck' has to stop. If Saturn points us to where we feel vulnerable and weak, it also points us to where we learn about ourselves through facing the weaknesses and attending to them. When we do, they become integrated with our lives as a whole and within them we may also find something of value and reward which raises us up. Thus its principles include constructiveness, perseverance, consolidation through experience and, importantly, clarification. Very often Saturn's position in the chart reflects the means by which a person can lead and teach others, having first faced in himself what needed to be faced, thus developing the responsibility and integrity to continue the learning process. Saturn is at once our weakest point, because we have suffered there, and our greatest gift, because we learn and grow through the suffering.

THE OUTER PLANETS: Uranus: Neptune: Pluto

As our obligation to clarify and learn about our limits and fears is met with Saturn, we can then move beyond its boundary to meet the three outermost planets known to man. We cannot bypass Saturn, but neither can we cling to the structure it offers nor hide behind its barriers. If we try to do so, we tend to draw rigid boundaries around ourselves, perhaps adopting oppressive 'laying-down-the-law' attitudes towards others; or, although we internalize our conscience with Saturn, we may escalate this to the point where we are forever addressing key questions to a sort of Internal Supervisor—a subpersonality within who may then delight in issuing a great many 'shoulds' and 'oughts' or 'better nots' beyond which we may never move to reach that key element of risk in our lives which makes us creative. Having learnt valuable lessons with Saturn, we then have to move through its portals and allow ourselves to step into something new.

This is where we meet **Uranus,** a herald who announces that things cannot stay the same—we have to move on, encounter changes, transform something in ourselves and in our lives, break  out of the constructs we have developed with Saturn—not do away with them altogether, but be prepared to open up a channel for something else to emerge. Uranus was discovered in 1781 and around that time it is pertinent to note that the world was experiencing this most central theme of change via three main revolutions—the American War of Independence, the French Revolution, which was close at hand and a third, though more subtle, revolution—the Industrial Revolution. Whatever had been held down, or kept rigid, oppressed or simply static, now sought change and broke out into a reversal of trends. Themes of discovery, innovation, the individuality of man, progressively transformed human experience and indeed became focused through a fourth kind of revolution, i.e., through the arts, for this was also leading up to the era of the revolutionary romanticists, the composers, painters, poets and writers whose works similarly evoked themes of innovation, man's individuality and his capacity for vision.

Discovery is in fact an important key to Uranus, for once we have passed Saturn we awaken to an even wider realm of the solar system where more is revealed. So, too, in the human individual Uranus correlates with the function deep within us that leads us to quite different facets of ourselves. The deeper core within us guides and beckons us on to integrate something new, something we did not know about before, into our conscious lives. Uranus is the traditional ruler of Aquarius, which in turn is the New Age we are now experiencing and which, as also mentioned earlier, has emphasized man's need to go beyond boundaries and find that there is very much more to him than that with which he consciously identifies. This is by no means always comfortable and change can, of course, be disruptive and upsetting. The tendency for many of us is to want to prevaricate or hang on to how things were before, to run back to the tested path of Saturn rather than risk the newness of Uranus, preferring the predictable to the erratic, the devil we know to the one we don't! Nevertheless, we do need to include Uranus in our lives (particularly at developmental periods where, as will be discussed later, it is in focus by transit or progression).

> Instead of snivelling about what is and has been, or inventing new sensations in the old line, it's got to break a way through, like a hole in the wall. And the public will scream and say it is a sacrilege: because, of course, when you've been jammed for a long time in a tight corner, and you get really used to its stuffiness and its tightness, till you find it suffocatingly cosy; then, of course, you're horrified when you see a new glaring hole in what was your cosy wall. You're horrified. You back away from the cold stream of fresh air as if it were killing you. But gradually, first one and then another of the sheep filters through the gap and finds a new world outside.
>
> (D. H. Lawrence, from *Phoenix*)

Although he was referring to the Novel in these lines, Lawrence's words might well apply to Uranus, for the way to handle change (or crisis) is to move through it and thus incorporate it as a turning point. Uranus is followed by Neptune in the solar system and, as we shall see later, an important function of Neptune within us is the inclusion and assimilation of all the bits and pieces left over from Uranus' eruption into changing what is outgrown. In astrological counselling, the position of Uranus in the birth chart is most noted by house and aspects, particularly if the latter involve the personal planets or Sun, Moon and Angles. Uranus remains in one sign for seven years and thus by zodiacal position is relevant to everyone born within this time span. Through Uranus, the counsellor is guided to an understanding of her client's capacity for originality or 'differentness', his individual and unique talents, or where he may display themes of 'encountering the new' via disruptive means, such as rebelliousness, erratic behaviour and attitudes, or strong independence. However expressed, the counsellor may be able to help the client discern what it is that is endeavouring to emerge from, for instance, the rebellion or the dynamism. With Uranus we can often use rebellion, or crisis, or any of the other themes, as a means of starting to awaken changes that invite expansion into our lives.

In the birth chart a person with, for instance, Sun in Cancer square to Uranus in Aries may be a creature of such habit (Cancer) that people look upon him as a kind of 'good old Fred', only to find that Uranus in Aries erupts at the most unlikely and outrageous moments and quite against their expectations. Through some kind of unexpected attitude he endeavours to remind those around him that he has some individuality and is not to be regarded as merely an habitual cog in an habitual machine chugging along the same grooves. The counsellor can help him understand this and discover what this individuality is trying to bring forward in his life. She can also help him to understand the Cancerian process underlying his investment in being 'good old Fred' and guide him, if it is appropriate to do so, into finding other ways of expressing his Arien Uranus if current ways prove upsetting to his emotional equilibrium (which may often be the case with the Cancerian Sun).

The nature of Uranus is also one of questioning, and in so doing it can often turn upside down static ways of looking at things. 'Why not?' it asks, and for those to whom cherished and tested ways or beliefs are important Uranus is regarded as the iconoclast. As such, and within the individual, its effect is sometimes shattering, but also often catalytic: it can be the sudden event that turns us hastily around on to a new path; it brings sharply to awareness the new idea, the new vision whose source is obscure; it can also be that which simply 'comes' to us—the letter you receive from your long-lost aunt in the Antipodes on the very day you have been thinking of her, the telephone call which somehow answers a query you have had rumbling inside you, the exciting flash of inspiration that can launch you into a new talent or skill, or the arresting moment of romantic attraction which shoots through you like a thousand volts! It is also the capacity you may have to bring a new idea into the world at large in galvanic ways that awaken people to the actuality of their lives.

As with Uranus, world conditions at the time when Neptune and Pluto were discovered throw light upon their significance. Neptune was discovered in 1846 and Pluto in 1930. At these times, the world was experiencing a desire to transcend the mundane and harsh in life, to reach for an ideal beyond (e.g. the emergence of the theosophical movement, the emancipation of slaves) and then an upsurge of that which sought to penetrate, eliminate and purge (e.g. the penetrating brutality of Nazi doctrine, but also exploration of the human psyche via development of searching psychoanalysis).

In meeting these planets, we are coming nearer to the outermost perimeter of our solar system—we have moved through the boundaries of Saturn and incorporated the new from Uranus; now with **Neptune** the journey continues and we long to reach the  ultimate universal experience of the entire sequence of planets. This, then, is the Neptune process—the longing, the yearning for something beyond the limits, beyond the disruptions, gossamer wings to take us beyond the fact that we are earthbound creatures. We seek the ideal, the ultimate, the spiritual—the utterly beautiful, utterly just, the divine, the absolute. Neptune is where we wish to dissolve into an ecstatic sense of oneness with all things, to revel in the fantastic, the glamorous, the ethereal, to find an enchanted paradise. Clearly, the process of Neptune can have as many problems as it does virtues.

In our bid to search for and attain final oneness with the Whole, we have choices. In wanting to create a better world, a world of beauty and perfect harmony, we may do something constructive and effective or we may batten down the hatches and escape into an inner fantasy world which shuts us off from the ugliness, pain or discouragement of our environment. So we may use Neptune as healers, guides, religious ministers, mystics: in prayer, meditation, to strive toward that which we call God: or we find Him through creating and appreciating beauty around us as artists—painters, poets, musicians, dancers, writers—and we attune ourselves to the wonder of things: of the earth, nature, a growing flower, an industrious ant—the miracle of each and every form of life living out its purpose in 'the entire scheme of things'.

On the other hand, we may do nothing effective at all, but simply dream of Utopia and fall asleep in front of the television in the process. Escape-routes can be many, including the over-consumption of alcohol, getting high on drugs, smoking too many cigarettes, or living life suspended in a void which removes us from a world which does not live up to our ideals. We become victims of one sort or another or go around saying things like 'if only . . .' and 'if it weren't for . . .' or 'wouldn't it be nice if . . .' and 'one day I'll . . .'. Sometimes, even if we do embark upon something which can add to the beauty, health and wholeness of the world, we may only live it through as a 'nine-day wonder'—it peters out into a Great Nothing, chaos, sham, confusion and we zero to the ground on very tattered wings. We may have reached too far for our ideal, too high for that picture of how and what we would like to be, and we find it hard to sustain the energy to reach such dreams. Then we might feel guilty and uncertain, or project our uncertainty and invite condemnation from others.

In astrological counselling we may look to Neptune to guide us to where the person is looking for his ultimate values in life. In this sense, Neptune may be regarded as Venus in higher manifestation. Neptune's values are those we need to strive to include and absorb, intangible though they may be. Even though we do not know what lies beyond Lawrence's 'hole in the wall', there is faith to lead us towards trust in a power beyond us, the Oneness of all things, the mystical, the divine—one path to which is the inner way of prayer and meditation.

For the person working with Neptunian energies in his life, we may need to help him build up this faith in what he feels to be ultimately meaningful. We may need to help him discover whether he might realistically find these ultimate values in the place he is looking, or whether the 'God' that he seeks is a fantasy, an idol. The partner may be idealized, or he may worship his job, his bank balance, his home, etc. These can also be in chaos and confusion, or the person may adopt an attitude of irresponsibility towards them on the grounds that something (or someone) will come along and rescue him. Neptune can often be an area where the person 'couldn't care less' and is content to let someone else worry about it, thus seeking to *ex*clude instead of *in*clude. He seeks a crutch to lean on, or he becomes a crutch for someone else.

Neptune can also be indicative of the need to sacrifice something —to be without, to let go. As such, it may be imbued with much experience of sadness, all-encompassing grief and feelings of guilt. It is frequently the case, for example, that an individual with Neptune contacting the personal planets has experienced some kind of loss in early life (such as a missing parent). There may be a great deal of guilt attached to this, with the individual feeling that perhaps they did something wrong or were bad children in some way; alternatively there is a general feeling of mistrust of, and abandonment by, a 'bad universe'. As a result, such individuals can often feel insecure in later life and unhappy at living on a planet which is less than ideal for them. Sometimes they strive to make up for these feelings of deficit by trying hard to be perfect, or by seeking perfection in another person (such as a marriage partner). If they have not known an absent parent, they may have built up a wonderful fantasy image of what he or she was like and then require the marriage partner to be that Ideal Person for them. Clearly it is a high demand, often an impossible demand, and the person may go painfully from one partner to another and then another, forever searching for the Wondrous—and forever let down, disillusioned, rejected. Sometimes also there is guilt in bringing up children single-handedly; in atonement, a parent may become totally self-sacrificial—ever-available for the innumerable demands of their offspring, even when the latter become adults. Or the person who has been over-showered with adoration as a child may in adult life require a partner who will similarly relate in a worshipping manner and thus sacrifice their own potential for maturity.

There are endless permutations of the basic Neptunian theme where the element of sacrifice attached to it is sadly lamented. Of course, an individual may also yield to it willingly as, for example, in those who choose a spiritual path above all others, shedding the shell of pure self-interest and satisfaction and reaching for an understanding and identification with all creation. Most often in astrological counselling, when a Neptunian process is in focus within the person's life, there is a need for him to relent in some way in order to gain something else, such as a new awareness. There may be a need to give up the search for an impossible ideal and mourn that it cannot be; or there is a general requirement to adjust, suspend, delay, be in limbo, hang fire—frequently because this kind of 'letting-go' enables us also to absorb something within ourselves which we may have been blind to before.

The process of Neptune is very subtle and yet can be powerful. Negatively, it may be experienced as invading, demanding, devious, insidious, corrosive. While living out an ostensible 'victim' role a person may be using his Neptune through manipulation, i.e. by portraying helplessness and hopelessness he may pull others in on a string to take care of things for him. Alternatively, he may seek to render others helpless by overwhelming them, always running around doing little things for them of which they are quite capable themselves, trying to smooth their worries and anxieties away (because he does not want to be troubled by their ugliness) or always apologizing for them and generally being quite odiously 'helpful'. Positively, Neptune can be experienced as inspiring, magical, miraculous, giving a sense of wonder and stillness with all life which heightens our inner understanding.

All of these themes, as principles of Neptune, may come to the surface in astrological counselling. Astrologers need to be aware of their own Neptunian element and ensure that they are not so bound up in heavenly considerations and ideals that they end up being no earthly use to the client; nor should they be so bound up with practical realities that they fail to understand the vision and faith of their client. They should also, of course, avoid being odiously helpful!

When we come to **Pluto** we reach the end of the sequence of planets; we have gone to the outermost planet we know. There may  be something beyond which is new again—a new planet, a new system, somewhere we can begin afresh. Thus 'the end' symbolizing a 'new beginning' are the themes of Pluto. We have moved through the hole in the wall; we may have screamed a lot at all of the fears, discomforts and insecurities our encounter with these nether regions of our being has led us to. Uranus within us invited and coaxed us to break free of fetters and see something new; Neptune within bribed us to descend even further into darker personal areas and catch a glimpse of our presence as part of a greater Universal Whole. Now Pluto insists that we undergo the end of a cycle. The chips are down and something must go, so that something entirely new can be born. Some kind of upheaval is necessary, for that deeper core of ours now takes us to all that we have held intact and bids us strip it away, to be transformed and regenerated. Whatever the situation we are outwardly dealing with in our lives—a relationship, a career, where we live, or whatever—all old habit patterns, beliefs, pretensions, all that we have clung to and become over-identified with have now to go; the old self dies and a new one appears. So Pluto symbolizes the inevitable cycle of death/rebirth which appears in all forms of life.

In astrological counselling, a person may be experiencing partial destruction or a crumbling of his existing set-up and complain that it is random or unjust. But by working with the counsellor to understand the principle of Pluto he may be guided into exploring how he can clear the way in his life for the new phase to start by this very elimination he is experiencing—getting rid of that which is superfluous and unnecessary to him now, the outdated, the untrue.

What we do with the Pluto within us is to take a sledgehammer to all of these things and release the new life, the new energy, trapped within them and waiting to be set free so that we can progress to an entirely new cycle in our lives. Sometimes this theme can emerge in our dreams; a woman with Pluto transiting in square aspect to her natal Sun had a dream in which a man entered her house and started to tear apart all the furniture with his bare hands. When she pleaded with him 'Well, couldn't we just salvage *this* chair, or *that* table . . . or maybe if we can just keep the handles off this wardrobe and use them for something else later on . . . or perhaps we could . . .' his reply was a steady 'Nope! It's all gotta go'. There are no half-measures with Pluto. We have to go along with that unconscious power which leads us to a new phase. If we do not, it takes hold of us by the scruff of the neck and insists that we do so, often by erupting into some powerful and intense experience. Nevertheless, tremendous care is needed in dealing with Pluto in the birth chart. Often a person may not be at a point where he can altogether cope with the deep issues Pluto can present and they often push up from the 'undergrowth' of our lives over an extended period of time, rather like the lengthy rumbling of a volcano before the energy is finally released. There is a distinct theme with Pluto of the past coming up to face us again—people known in the past, old family ties, roots, memories. A consciousness of things past can suddenly emerge and we are ambushed into dealing with them. More especially, that which lies *unresolved* in the past can flood into the conscious mind and very often extended counselling over a period of time and/or deeper forms of psychotherapy are more appropriate —certainly when one considers that for some, beyond the first small fissures of the volcano, unfathomable depths of lava may be waiting to emerge.

In the birth chart, Pluto is regarded by house position and contact with personal planets and angles. A Mars/Pluto conjunction, for instance, combines action (Mars) with Pluto's theme of brute strength and power. Sometimes this can be experienced as some very deep anger inside with which the client may show a need to get in touch, even though he may not be able to express it in his day-to-day life. If so, it may be appropriate for the astrological counsellor to suggest some way in which he can enact his feelings in a safe and supported situation, such as through psychodrama, and having released the energy pent-up within he may redirect it in creative ways—Mars/Pluto intensified strength of action can, also, for instance be the stuff that North Pole explorers are made of. Or a person may sublimate the energy of Pluto in some way—a friend of mine with Pluto transiting in opposition to an angular Mars in Aries a few years ago went out and bought himself a powerful motorbike! Thankfully, he kept his own safety well in mind. We need also to remember that Pluto's energy may be used by a person to hold intact and under an iron cover something which is painful inside. A very powerful, dictatorial, bullying or threatening person may be using such behaviour to harbour an inner feeling of worthlessness or inadequacy. Since the cover has been placed there by the person in order to make his life tolerable, extreme care is needed in approaching it and assessing its potential for removal. Collusion with the covering up of these inner feelings can also lead to an unhealthy increase of their grip, which the astrological counsellor also needs to be aware of.

Although Pluto has a correlation with our need for intense and powerful experiences that will pitch us into new channels for self-understanding and progress, when we are going through these phases in our lives we also need to remind ourselves of the 'new beginning'. Power lies in that embryo and, as mentioned before, embryos need care and attention; if not they will abort. When Pluto emerges from within, it can understandably feel right at first to cast ourselves headlong into the fray; but whatever is dredged up from within to be dealt with also holds the new and viable. This can be very clear at a time when Pluto is transiting, say, Venus. With this transit a person may become aware, for instance, that his current personal relationship is not what he requires—perhaps he does not feel loved enough or appreciated; perhaps the relationship is failing to help him grow psychologically. At any rate, let us say that he becomes aware that it is crumbling—either a little or a lot—and may have been for some little time past. Perhaps he then meets another person to whom he feels he could relate more positively; then his original set-up feels even more as if it is crumbling. After a while, he might either decide to play 'not at home' to Pluto and refuse to look at his feelings and relating patterns at all, remaining in the old familiar situation, treading the same, albeit crumbling, path; or he may decide to leave and start the relationship with the new person, but he does so obsessively (the intense power of Pluto). In choosing the first option, the surging unconscious power requiring him to strip away that which is outworn is now denied an outlet and has to find another route to make its existence known (if he is really 'not at home' to it, he may become ill for instance). In the second option (taking on the new relationship) the obsession cannot be sustained for it is not given adequate nurturing and thus, after its first magnificence, it aborts.

By tapping the essence of Pluto's message, we may understand more clearly not only what is required, but how we may best master and handle crucial phases which call us to transform our lives, to create them anew. For the Venus/Pluto person, it may well be that neither leaving his current relationship nor creating a new one is required, but that something within his existing relationship is negative and drastically needs attention. He may be guided into taking a breathing space to look at all that his relating patterns have held in the past, to explore the remoter regions Pluto leads him to so that these past patterns can be transmuted and redeemed. If he does decide that a new relationship is what he needs, the transformative work he does on his feelings and needs will provide a healthy preliminary and avoid the risk of him grafting old patterns onto the new relationship and the new partner.

This, then, marks some of the essence of what the counsellor can help the client reach to through Pluto, to plumb the process and purpose of what he is dealing with.

6.
THE CYCLE OF THE ZODIAC AND THE ELEMENTS

For most people, there is a tendency toward thinking of the zodiacal signs both as twelve separate categories and also as designations of specific characteristics (Aries is aggressive, Scorpio is jealous, Pisces confused, and so on). On both these scores, it seems to me, the point is rather missed. First of all, the cycle of signs *is* in fact a cycle and, as such, each stage in the overall sequence of twelve follows a logical progression; therefore each of the signs has a link with those preceding and following it. Each sign is one stage and constitutes an integral part of an entire cyclic path. It needs to be regarded from the central standpoint of what its position within the cycle seeks to impart to that cycle as a whole in order to render it complete.

Secondly (and importantly in astrological counselling), the bestowal of definite characteristics to each sign hinders us from identifying the basic principle underlying it, and from which these characteristics have been derived in the first place. By continuing to speak of such-and-such a sign in terms of character diagnosis, we are in danger of overlooking the essential function the person has to fulfil through the sign; additionally, we may be quite at a loss when we meet someone of that sign who does not display precisely the characteristics we have neatly assigned to it.

In this respect, an important function of the astrological counsellor is to know that characteristics ascribed to different signs are but a few of the possible manifestations of what are, first of all, fundamental human energies, qualities and life principles. So that,

LIBRA

CARDINAL: AIR
RULER: ♀

Process: Establishing relationships on equal footing with others and then on to (process of ♏)...

Theme: Co-operation

Manifests as: Meditation, diplomacy, tact, discretion, equality, justice, fairness, negotiation, umpiring, need for 'niceness', appearance, social acceptability, wavering, 'laissez faire', indecisive, pleasant, harmonising.

SCORPIO

FIXED: WATER
RULERS: ♂ ♇

Process: Deeper intensification of relating to others, building commitment, in interpersonal relationships which leads to (process of ♐)...

Theme: Intensity

Manifests as: Penetrating, incisive, thorough, deep commitment, passionate, possessive of relationships, involvement, persistence, depth, getting to the 'nub', achievement of ends, 'cutting', 'stinging', investigation, acute, insistent.

SAGITTARIUS

MUTABLE: FIRE
RULER: ♃

Process: Opening up a wider scope of relating to the world at large, moving further afield having expanded horizons, then (process of ♑)...

Theme: Exploration

Manifests as: Adventurous, explorative, carefree, roaming, need for wide berth, unconcerned with results, restless, seeking new horizons, travelling (both physically and mentally), philosophical, wide experience, understanding, brash, exaggerative.

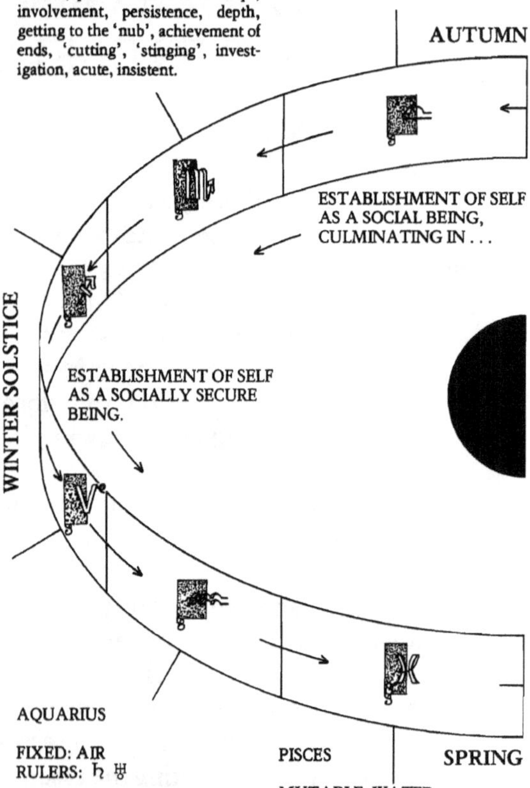

CAPRICORN

CARDINAL: EARTH
RULER: ♄

Process: Establishment of social base, creating a structured 'platform' which then becomes a leverage point for (process of ♒)...

Theme: Responsibility

Manifests as: Clarification of order, constancy, self-discipline, control, direction, tolerance, hard-work, solidarity, stern, propriety, duty, seriousness, aloneness, ambition, superiority, conforming, 'putting one's house in order', managerial.

AQUARIUS

FIXED: AIR
RULERS: ♄ ♅

Process: Giving way of structures to introduce progress, social creativity, leading to (process of ♓)...

Theme: Innovation

Manifests as: Progressive ways, inventive, reforming, original, breakaway, non-conformist, impersonal, man with a mission, remote, aloof, wilful imposition of the new, challenging, dynamic, forward-looking, unconcerned, detached, objective.

PISCES

MUTABLE: WATER
RULERS: ♃ ♆

Process: Culmination, completion and transcendence of one complete cycle, leading to commencement of another (process of ♈)...

Theme: Reflection/Dissolution

Manifests as: Receptivity, sensitivity, impressionability, sacrificial, drifting, searching for belief, dreamer, impractical, romantic, tentative, muddled, subtle, manipulative, fantasy, needing to save, rescue, vision, immersion into experience, lack of clarity, need for escape, emotional overwhelm.

AUTUMN

ESTABLISHMENT OF SELF AS A SOCIAL BEING, CULMINATING IN...

WINTER SOLSTICE

ESTABLISHMENT OF SELF AS A SOCIALLY SECURE BEING.

SPRING

Figure 3. The Cycle of the Zodiac.

VIRGO

MUTABLE: EARTH
RULER: ☿

Process: Need to improve self, assess own development and give recognition to others through rendering service, and thus (process of ♎)...

Theme: **Discrimination**

Manifests as: Systematic, analytical, quick, comprehension, able to sort, sieve, estimate, discern, compare, contrast, administer, concern for welfare of others, obliging, gathering results of past endeavours and learning/teaching therefrom, detailed, worrying, need for order/detail, pedantic.

EQUINOX

LEO

FIXED: FIRE
RULER: ☉

Process: Display oneself as a creative individual, achieve recognition which then leads to (process of ♍)...

Theme: **Self-Promotion**

Manifests as: Radiance, warmth, 'show', flamboyance, grandiosity, drama, 'on stage', autocratic, exhibition, 'royal', commanding, masterful, magnanimity, generosity, fun, laughter, play, 'shine', haughty, 'big' ways.

CANCER

CARDINAL: WATER
RULER: ☽

Process: Emergence of a sense of emotional base, identifying one's own niche, emotionally secure enough to (process of ♌)...

Theme: **Emotional Belonging**

Manifests as: Protective, vulnerable, sensitive, nostalgic, caring, nurturing, devoted, need for familiarity, habit-patterns, tenacious, safety-seeking, withdrawal, clinging.

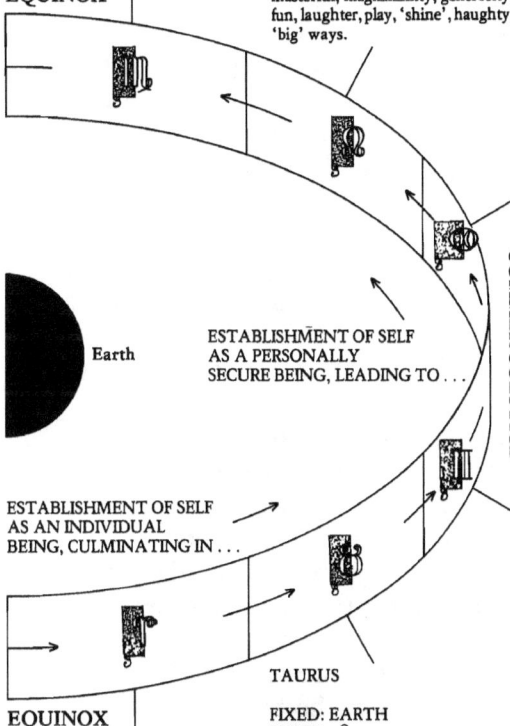

Earth

ESTABLISHMENT OF SELF AS A PERSONALLY SECURE BEING, LEADING TO...

SUMMER SOLSTICE

ESTABLISHMENT OF SELF AS AN INDIVIDUAL BEING, CULMINATING IN...

GEMINI

MUTABLE: AIR
RULER: ☿

Process: Discovery can begin of the environment in which experience takes place, acquaintance with the milieu, and having done so (process of ♋)...

Theme: **Mobility**

Manifests as: Curiosity, restlessness, inquisitive, inconsistent, quick, agile, versatile, 'chatty', communicative, connecting links.

EQUINOX

ARIES

CARDINAL: FIRE
RULER: ♂

Process: First onrush on energy to initiate new cycle of experience, leading to (process of ♉)...

Theme: **Propulsive Energy**

Manifests as: Assertion, aggression, impulsiveness, rashness, recklessness, crusader principles, courage, pugnacity, enterprise, adventure, risk-taking, hot-blooded, go-getting, indiscriminate, selfishness, spur to achieve, 'pushy'.

TAURUS

FIXED: EARTH
RULER: ♀

Process: Maintenance of new phase started by underpinning with available resources rendering secure so that (process of ♊)...

Theme: **Maintenance**

Manifests as: Solid, sure, reliable, steadfast, resourceful, slow, careful, deliberate, endurance, obstinacy, possession-oriented, industrious, conservative, 'testing the water'.

instead of telling the Sun in Aries person that he is aggressive, pushy, reckless or courageous, she will describe for him the essential *process* and *theme* of the sign and through their conversation together will help him clarify how he lives these out in his life. She may, of course, make suggestions as to the possible ways it can emerge, and it might actually turn out that the client is living it out by being aggressive, pushy, reckless, etc! But counselling is not about labelling people and putting them into compartments. When dealing with the signs, the counsellor should always be ready to hear her client's view and experience of himself, as well as fostering insights which can help him connect to the process more easily.

There is another twofold point concerning the signs which may be helpful (particularly for the newcomer to astrology), which is (a) although one may be designated, say, 'a Gemini', this is because the Sun occupied that particular sign at the time of birth (as it did for countless numbers of other people), but the complete, personal chart will hold a strong focus on other signs as well; and (b) even though one may not be 'a Gemini', nevertheless wherever Gemini appears in the birth chart (and we all have this sign somewhere), in that area of life the person will need to develop and draw on the essence of Gemini. The 'ruler' of the sign (the planet which has most affinity with it) will give further guidance as to the best ways for him to do so.

In *Figure 3*, the signs are shown in their position within the cycle of twelve, together with descriptions of the principles, drives and needs intrinsic to each, and with each sign's process building from and on to its adjacent signs. Any verbal definitions can only portray a taste of possible meanings, which is why, in astrological counselling, it is via dialogue with the client that the clearer meaning of it *for him* can be reached. Of first importance is for the client to be allowed to relate to that principle, or process, as he lives and experiences it, for it is the human being who brings the *general* principle of a planet or sign to *specific* life.

Figure 4 shows how planets and signs are written astrologically and may be referred to when these symbols are used in the text.

By way of example (if the reader will forgive the inconsistency of starting with the fourth sign of the zodiac instead of the first), we can see from *Figure 3* that a basic principle and theme at the Cancer stage is the need to establish a sense of belonging. Whether one does this by being home-loving, nurturing or any of those other characteristics commonly assigned to Cancer we do not know specifically until we talk with the person.

THE SIGNS OF THE ZODIAC

ARIES	♈	LIBRA	♎
TAURUS	♉	SCORPIO	♏
GEMINI	♊	SAGITTARIUS	♐
CANCER	♋	CAPRICORN	♑
LEO	♌	AQUARIUS	♒
VIRGO	♍	PISCES	♓

THE PLANETS

SUN	☉	JUPITER	♃
MOON	☽	SATURN	♄
MERCURY	☿	URANUS	♅
VENUS	♀	NEPTUNE	♆
MARS	♂	PLUTO	♇

Figure 4. Astrological Glyphs

Mr W. was born with four planets in Cancer. The astrologer could tell him he is home-loving, sensitive, moody and nurturing but she might very well be met with a blank stare. Instead she describes for him the underlying principles of the sign and explains how, as a theme, it will in some way underline his life experience. Mr W. has previously told her that he is a department head in a company, a position he has held for many years. He is comfortable and content in his work, but recently a merger with another company has been discussed and this is 'bothering' him. He has been told, and feels assured, that he will not lose his job but nevertheless, although he cannot pinpoint why, he feels bothered. At the following point in their conversation together, Mr W. and the astrological counsellor (who is also bearing in mind that Uranus is approaching Mr W's Midheaven by transit) have been discussing the sign Cancer:

Mr W: A sense of belonging ... yes that's true really. I suppose that's what I do look for. I mean, thinking what you've

	described about Cancer, I think this has really been through my work. As I said, I'm comfortable in the job and I'm used to it. I suppose that's what makes me feel so bothered about this merger that's happening.
Cllr:	Do you feel threatened by it?
Mr W:	In a way I suppose I do. Oh, I don't think I'll lose my job —in fact I *know* I won't, as I said . . . but . . . well . . . [*tails off*].
Cllr:	But there'll be changes.
Mr W:	Yes, oh yes, there'll be changes, and I'm used to the people I've got working around me and the way things are done . . . I don't really like the thought of . . . oh I don't know.
Cllr:	Hmm . . . is it that you don't want new people coming in and doing things in different ways?
Mr W:	That's right, I've worked hard in my job and I'm used to the people—I guess I'm pretty clannish really [*pauses*]—yes, clannish I suppose.
Cllr:	Yes, I see. It must be a bit like your own 'family' of people you've got around you and . . . [*interrupted*]
Mr W.	Well, I was just thinking it's more like . . . well, it sounds daft I suppose, but it's more like my lifeboat that gets me through the waters of life . . . I know I won't get turned out of the boat but . . . [*pauses*]
Cllr:	But you don't want anyone else to come on board.
Mr W:	Yes, exactly. Yes, I suppose I like to keep things as they are . . . well, familiar.

The client has clarified for himself what the 'nub' of the bother is. The basic process of Cancer has been explained to him but by being spared *set* interpretations of its manifestation in his life, he has been able to explore his own experience of it and decide that his pattern of keeping things (and people) familiar is most at the base of his drive to achieve a sense of belonging. From this point, he and the counsellor are more in a relationship of co-operation which can enable the session to progress further towards opening up the relevance of the Uranus transit and what may be trying to emerge within Mr W. at this time. The process of Uranus, as we have seen, is one in which that which has been familiar needs to encounter something which is new. If he has been living cocooned within the Cancer process he may now need to embrace some changes and break out of the pattern of keeping things familiar. It may be that he needs to relinquish this altogether and lift himself out of what may have become a 'rut' into something entirely new; or perhaps, although he has been told he will not lose his job, he is feeling deep down that this might not be so. These are all possibilities which can form the basis of continued conversation with the client.

It is also relevant that Mr W. has been able to connect freely with the element of Water (the Water signs being Cancer, Scorpio and Pisces), which associates with feeling. Mr W. just *feels* bothered and cannot pinpoint a logical 'why'. For the Water signs, the heart has its reasons. Additionally, his analogy of a lifeboat clearly centres him on this path along which he has developed and which, again, he is being required to reflect upon as Uranus approaches his Midheaven.

Jackie, a young girl with Sun conjunct Venus in Libra (with their themes of needing to experience that which is pleasing, agreeable, co-operative, personal and social appreciation), knew enough about astrology to have set up her own chart and be familiar with the basics of interpretation. She came with the following feeling of conflict between two sets of chart factors:

Jackie: Well, I wanted to talk over things about my career—well, such as it is . . . I haven't really got one—I'm not really sure which direction to go in.

Cllr: You've no idea of what you want to do, or is there a general line you've got in mind?

Jackie: Well, general, yes. You see, I'd like something, I suppose its Libra really, something to do with fashion, or jewellery . . . make-up . . . that sort of thing.

Cllr: Yes, I see—you like pretty things, beauty and . . .

Jackie: Beauty, yes—beauty therapy interests me a lot [*Jackie goes on to talk about women who work as Beauty Consultants in large stores, and courses on beauty therapy she has seen advertisements for*].

Cllr: Well, yes. As you say, that does seem to be very much these Libran planets here [*chart is in front of them*]—so what's the problem? Getting started?

Jackie: Yes, I think that's what it is, but I'm pulled, you see. I went to another astrologer a few weeks ago and he told me I should take up teaching. I think he was going by my Virgo rising and this strong Mercury [*points to chart*].

Cllr: I see, and you think that might be another possibility.

Jackie: No . . . well, yes . . . I mean, no . . . well . . . [*both smile, then Jackie starts again*]. Well, what I mean is the thought of going into a classroom and kids and all that . . .

Cllr: Oh, I see, teaching children.

Jackie: Well, what other kind is there?

Cllr: I was just hearing it as a suggestion you'd taken up about teaching children in school—was that what your previous astrologer suggested?

Jackie: Well, I presume so. I hadn't thought really . . . I don't . . . [*tails off*].

Cllr: [*pause*]. So you've got two possibilities—teaching of some kind, and beauty therapy, or fashion or any of the other things you mentioned.

Jackie: Yes, but I like the idea of beauty therapy *more*.

Cllr: So how are you feeling pulled?

Jackie: Sorry?

Cllr: You said earlier you were feeling pulled . . .

Jackie: Oh, yes. Well, I was just wondering, I don't really

	understand that Virgo bit of my chart—I mean teaching seems to go with it, but if I don't use it that way I don't know how else I use it.
Cllr:	What would you like to do in beauty therapy—I mean presumably you'd train in it and you've got some information on courses? [*Jackie nods*] and then what would . . .
Jackie:	Well then I'd like to get a job perhaps demonstrating or work in a salon, you know somewhere I could get lots of practical experience. There's quite a lot to find out about all the different aspects of make-up, skin care and all those things.
Cllr:	Yes, I would imagine so—and all of that sounds very Virgo don't you think? Training, getting information, practical experience, demonstration . . . very often, wherever Virgo is in our charts, we use it in some kind of apprenticeship way, where we learn through practice and experie . . .
Jackie:	Oh, yes, yes, of course. I suppose . . . well it would really be a blend of Libra and Virgo wouldn't it.
Cllr:	Yes, and again often the Virgo theme of providing a service contains an element of learning and teaching at the same time . . .

★   ★   ★   ★   ★

As mentioned earlier, sometimes people will experience planetary/zodiacal themes in another person prior to understanding them as part of their own make-up.

Brian has Venus and Mars in Aries (I desire, I want— ♀ now, immediately— ♂♈) and both these planets are on the Descendant. The second time he and the counsellor meet, he is discussing a difficulty he is having in his relationship with his wife:

Brian:	You know, Vicki's very selfish [*Vicki is Brian's wife*]. Perhaps I shouldn't say that, it seems unfair [*Brian has Libra on the Ascendant*], but, well she is.

Cllr: In what ways?

Brian: Well, I mean—take the other day for instance. She wanted me to redecorate the hall. Well, it's a large house we've got and that would take ★★★ [*expletive*]*ages* and she just expects me to do it there and then, no matter what else I've got on hand. It's *so* selfish... it's not as if it *needs* doing.

Cllr: So you felt it was a bit much to ask [*Brian nods*]. And what happened? Did you do it?

Brian: ★★★ no! And not only that, she wanted me to do it in this green colour—she *even* had the ★★★ colour all lined up! [*We all use charged language when complaining of something in another person which may also lie within ourselves!*]

Cllr: Did you not want to do it at all, or was it that you'd rather she'd talked it over with you?

Brian: Well, I must say I think a paler colour, a blue or something would be much better. Anyway, we had an argument. I *told* her I had a lot on at the factory and I can't just drop everything just like that. Anyway, the upshot was I'm doing it on the Bank Holiday instead [*screws his eyes together and looks upwards to the ceiling*]. I think I've got some pale blue somewhere... maybe in the attic [*comes back to the conversation again*]. Anyway, it was a fight I can tell you...

Cllr: Brian, it may well be that Vicki *is* being very demanding, but would you find it surprising if I said that these things you've been describing in Vicki have to do with themes in your chart?

Brian: Uh? Well... how do you mean?

Cllr: [*Explains the principles of Venus and Mars in Aries mentioned earlier*]... and they're in a part of the chart which represents where we often meet qualities, traits, and so on, in other people, particularly people who are close to us, when they are also part of our own nature... that's often the way we first get to know about them in

THE CYCLE OF THE ZODIAC AND THE ELEMENTS   71

ourselves. That doesn't mean that Venus and Mars in Aries are selfish fullstop—basically, the process of them is go-getting, assertive, with an eye to immediate needs and going straight to them—I'd think for instance this would be very much what you do in your job [*focusing on Pluto, which is also tied in by aspect and knowing that Brian has built up the factory of which he spoke earlier and is Managing Director*].

Brian: Yes, well, yes I do—but I don't think I get my own way with things like Vicki . . . except I suppose I *am* doing the hall on the Bank Holiday . . .

Cllr: In pale blue . . . [*gives a small smile*].

Brian: Ye-e . . . mmh . . . Yes, I see . . . [*smiles too which disperses the tension and enables them to continue the conversation openly*].

★ ★ ★ ★ ★

Sometimes, as also mentioned earlier, planetary and zodiacal themes can come across in conversations with people concerning their parents and what they were like, and there is often something of an 'action replay' when it comes to choosing a marriage partner.

Sarah, with a conglomeration of planets in Aquarius opposed by Pluto in Leo, has been talking about themes of an impersonal kind of power in her relationships and about her husband, who 'never reacts to anything'.

Cllr: You can't get through to him?

Sarah: Yes, bit like my father really.

Cllr: Uh huh?

Sarah: Yes, Dad always presented himself as the Good Guy, very easy going and good natured. Mum was the one who ran around making waves and having tantrums, but Dad . . . well, its difficult really, because he doesn't relate except in a neighbourly chatty kind of way. He's the local dentist and he's had this practice for years and years and he knows everyone—everyone's friendly

	neighbourhood dentist, and he's got a sort of 'patter'. And he's mad about cars... he'd rather be with *things*.
Cllr:	A patter?
Sarah:	Yes, I remember going into his surgery once and he was just finishing with a patient when I got there. I waited outside and as I sat there I just thought quite flippantly 'Oh there goes Pa with his patter'. Oh, it's all so inconsequential and punctuated by little laughs and everything, you know the sort of patter, and then out comes the patient and they're terribly thrilled [*Counsellor nods*]... I mean I think he was very good with people, and they went back to him year after year, but at a certain level there was a certain distance—and then when I went in after this patient had gone he started talking to me in exactly the same way, the same patter, the weather and so on. And I just said naively 'Dad, y'know, it's me... Sarah... it's *me*—you're coming over with the same patter'—and he just said 'Oh yes, well y'know dear, blah, blah'... and he just carried on!
Cllr:	So your father lived in a role, rather than...
Sarah:	Yes. Very much so, *very* much so. And I think he lived like that most of... no, *all* the time.
Cllr:	That sounds rather sad.
Sarah:	I suppose it is. I don't feel sad... I just feel... well, I don't know... I mean my father was so *unknown*—that can drive you crazy actually.
Cllr:	Mmm. It hasn't driven you crazy though. But maybe you're feeling angry?
Sarah:	Yes, when I look at Bob [*her husband*] and our relationship—yes, I am aware of feeling a helluva lot of anger... I don't really know what it's about except that in some vague kind of way it has to do with men and their power.
Cllr:	I don't know the answer to that either, but what seems to be coming clear is that your father appears to have

THE CYCLE OF THE ZODIAC AND THE ELEMENTS   73

been in the Good Guy role, the one who never puts a foot wrong and says all the right things. And mother on the other hand is running around making waves and having tantrums. Maybe you could have felt angry at the power your father held . . . I mean by withholding—if he lived in a role, maybe he *withheld* really relating to you as a person? Or maybe you felt you wanted to make a dent in his Good Guy image?

Sarah: I think the withholding . . . [*pause*] . . . yes . . . [*pause*] . . . do you know I never fully realized the power of someone who withholds like my father . . . and Bob too . . . and it's [*frowns*] . . . well now it's . . . [*pause*] . . . well, I do it . . . [*slowly*] . . . I do it myself. I'm thinking of something that happened last week . . . when *I* did this myself . . . it's very . . . the power of withholding . . . [*thinking deeply*].

Ross is an advertising executive whose pace of work is hotting up and he feels unable to cope sometimes. He has been collecting criticism from others in the agency where he works for not dealing with main issues, but wasting time on things that do not really matter and usually everything ends up as a rush job because of this. Sun, Mercury and Venus are in Virgo, Mars is in Leo, and there is also a focal Neptune in the chart. Ross has also studied some astrology:

Ross: I suppose it's what the books talk about as Virgo being 'pernickety'—I mean the others are always saying how I take too much time over tiny little things when there's some major account to be dealt with. Is that what it is? Is Virgo always like that?

Cllr: No, not at all. But seizing on minute issues could be a sort of steady timing mechanism you might adopt with Virgo to ensure that every small thing has been properly marshalled before harnessing the Mars in Leo to deal with the major job [*Mars in Leo is potentially very dynamic energy but the strong Neptune may also introduce feelings of uncertainty in Ross*].

Ross: Isn't that quite a sensible thing to do though?

Cllr: Oh yes, certainly. But maybe what the others are worried about is that you may never get to the Mars in Leo, do you think? Or that when you do it's usually a last-minute mad rush for everyone.

Ross: I expect so, I don't really know . . . [*trails off*].

Cllr: [*Endeavours to lead into possible Neptunian uncertainty which Ross's situation may contain*]. I don't know if this helps Ross, but sometimes with Mercury and Venus in Virgo, which are the drives we have to think things out, to decide, to evaluate, well, in Virgo it can be rather like a 'stacker' system at Heathrow or something. The control tower of Virgo may often prefer to bring in the little two-seater aircraft before going on to Concorde as it were . . . the 'biggie'! [*endeavouring to focus on whether Ross really prefers not to have to deal with major issues in his job, but only day-to-day routines*].

Ross: Oh yeah, exactly . . . yes.

Cllr: . . . which can be OK, but as long as Concorde isn't kept circling above so long it runs out of fuel to complete its landing?

Ross: Yes [*pauses*]. It's the finality of that landing I guess . . . I just put it off for as long as I can.

Cllr: Then it has to make an emergency landing? [*which then leads Ross into having to cope with the rush job*].

Ross: Yes, that's it. Everything's then Urgent Priority—*chaos*!

Cllr: So it's a bit of a three-cornered hat, really. Your Virgo planets probably don't like chaos, huh? [*Ross nods*] But I'm wondering . . . well, do you think, Ross, that the Urgent Priority might hold a bit of excitement for Mars in Leo? And then there's the Neptune we talked about earlier.

Ross:	I guess on some level . . . well, I suppose I might get a kick out of it . . . but the Neptune yes, that's what I feel most . . . I get so worried that everything's going to go wrong. I think that's why I avoid it so much.
Cllr:	So, do you think the high drama of it might be something you get yourself into to ensure that people will come and rescue [*interrupted*].
Ross:	[*Big sigh*] . . . Yeah . . . it's like a ★ ★ ★ insurance policy that . . . yeah, leaving it all to the last minute, creating the drama so that other people, yeah—that's it.

Taking out an 'insurance policy' against fear of failure seemed to be what Ross most identified with and this enabled him to explore where this fear lay, which in turn may enable him to open up other, more satisfying ways, of using these planetary and zodiacal energies.

★ ★ ★ ★ ★

Carol, who knows a great deal about astrology, is talking about her Moon in Scorpio in the eighth house (the natural house of Scorpio) in its negative aspect:

Carol:	Oh sure, I've had a lot of problems with this through typical manifestations of intense rage, even jealous rage . . . yes, quite destructive. I mean I remember when I was living with someone and after we broke up I saw him with two other women. I got into such a furious rage, I just sat in my flat and just ripped this pair of jeans I had to *shreds*. Then I smashed against the kitchen door, just kicking and kicking for about ten minutes . . . and then I just cried and cried and cried. After that, well I walked around for about half an hour just to get rid of it. And I don't let things *alone*, I won't let things *be* . . . it's as if I make things as painful as possible for myself emotionally . . . and if someone leaves me for another woman I feel she must be better than me in some way . . . I go through this intense jealousy—afterwards I usually feel sick with remorse about it all.

★ ★ ★ ★ ★

Sometimes it helps people to be able to think in terms of 'subpersonalities' for different features of their charts in order to connect with the varying behaviours, feelings, patterns of thought and moods in their lives. These are other little selves inside who come into play in different situations and there can be very many of them, some of whom are helpful and some a nuisance! Some we may give a great deal of attention to, others we barely acknowledge at all. We can give names to these subpersonalities, such as Little Girl Lost, or Bully, Tycoon, Harrassed Housewife, Cynic, Hollywood Star, Playboy . . . .

Sally has taken part in psychology training workshops, which have helped her locate some of her subpersonalities, which she talks about to the astrological counsellor. In Sally's chart there is a strong emphasis upon Moon in Cancer, the signs Sagittarius and Aries, and also a strong Saturn. Sally has identified 'Tragic Woman', who is always burdened with one problem or another (which is how Sally has used her Saturn), 'Crybaby' (☽ ♋)* who really wants to stay safe at home in her own little cocooned world and, lately, 'Monte Carlo Dazzler' (♐ ♈), who loves travelling, excitement, freedom and risk-taking. Faced with the offer of an exciting job which would mean a lot of travelling for her, Sally said:

> Most of all I'm thrilled to bits. Monte Carlo Dazzler is saying things like 'Wow, this is *great*! but those other two you know . . . boy, they drag me down. And the trouble is, well, I'm so used to them I may be allowing them too much rein. Crybaby is saying things like 'Boo hoo, I'm too small and weak for this job and people might not be nice to me, I don't feel safe', and as for Tragic Woman, well she goes on and on, with her chin set high in the air, about 'I am alone, bereft and eternally burdened. I have never been fulfilled in my work and altogether have a tragic life— I am to be admired for my resilience in the face of such suffering' . . . Can you imagine!

The essence of the subpersonalities we carry within us are remarkably well depicted in our astrological charts and the counsellor who is familiar with this concept can help the client

---

*For planetary and zodiacal symbols, see *Figure 4.*, p 65.

listen closely and give attention to what each requires and has to offer. She can similarly point the client in the direction of further ways of working with these concepts so that the central core of the person can, in such situations as Sally was experiencing, be realigned to its main path and achieve equilibrium amongst the many selves surrounding it.

THE ASTROLOGICAL ELEMENTS:
Fire: Earth: Air: Water

Following on from the division of the zodiacal belt into twelve signs, astrology makes further division into these four elements, as follows:

FIRE—Aries, Leo and Sagittarius
EARTH—Taurus, Virgo and Capricorn
AIR—Gemini, Libra and Aquarius
WATER—Cancer, Scorpio and Pisces

These are representative of the ways in which human beings apprehend and experience their world and are taken note of by the astrological counsellor in differentiating the variable lines along which people develop. The elements have been very clearly covered by two astrological writers in particular whose works appear in the appendix to this book (Stephen Arroyo and Liz Greene), but for the purpose of brief synopsis here we may say that the **Water** signs follow a general line of development based on subjective experience. Their criterion is value and this is what their judgements are based upon—something is worthy or not, or right or not, because that is how it feels (as in the case of Mr W.). In the astrological Water signs the essential composition is that of fluidity, of feeling, which (like the ocean) can contain great depths. Hence the sensitivity of Cancer, whereby we seek an interior sense of belonging; the passion and committment of Scorpio, through which we relate by subjecting ourselves to a very intense level of feeling; the amorphous receptivity of Pisces, where we are open to the indivisibility of the entire cycle as a twelvefold totality of experience, just as twelve months within four seasons (and vice-versa) is one cycle of a year, leading us on to another.

The **Air** signs follow a line of development based on judgement through tracing causes and reasons. In these signs we assess whether and how things can be from the point of view of logic. Their composition is one in which factors are linked together in movement and communication, like air blowing around us and communicating sound. With Gemini we are curious, mobile, inquisitive concerning that which is around us; in Libra we are seeking to weigh one thing against another and to link up with others in social participation; with our Aquarian energies we observe and assess both past and present for the purpose of communicating new ideas for the future.

The **Earth** signs follow a concrete line of development based on external facts. They enable us to state what is, or what is not, according to what we can see, hear, touch, smell, and which we register automatically. The composition of these signs is of efficiency, order, practicality—the solid, steady resourcefulness of Taurus, the systematic improvement and ordered analysis of Virgo, the purposeful responsibility and 'platform' of Capricorn.

The **Fire** signs follow an impromptu and unrehearsed development, one that is based on conjecture, in which we open ourselves to the possibility of things to come. Thus, their composition is rather like leaping or flickering flames—spontaneous, powerful and active. Our Arien energies are those which enable us to be assertive, enthusiastic, undirected yet nevertheless bounding onward; with Leo we are radiant, creative, aglow in our self-display, and with Sagittarius we are forever exploring, both near and far, horizons which to us hold promise of new possibilities, that which is impending, a sense of 'getting warmer'.

Catherine, who we will meet again later and who has Sun square Saturn and Virgo rising (an emphasis on Earth energies), has a small son who has an emphasis of planets in Fire signs. As can be deduced from the outlines of the elements above, while the Earth signs are practical and orderly, Fire signs live in a world of unpremeditated action and intangible meanings:

Catherine: You know, Paul's—well, I feel he doesn't know what to do with himself and I feel stuck because I don't know how to help him. I mean Christopher [*Catherine's eldest son*] is crazy about football and wants to join the Boys

THE CYCLE OF THE ZODIAC AND THE ELEMENTS 79

Club and all the sort of stuff boys of his age normally do, but Paul's sort of wandering around inside himself and I get very worried because I feel [*sighs*] . . . there's a tremendous sense of just thrashing around and not knowing what to . . ., I . . . I feel there's something there inside him, I know there is, something individual, and I feel I should be the one to give him some . . . well, I don't know really . . .

Cllr: Is it that you feel this kind of thrashing and wandering around inside him needs a direction, or are you feeling it needs to be held down? [*both are possibilities for Catherine's Sun/Saturn function*].

Catherine: Oh I don't . . . tch! [*Big sigh*]—there may be a bit of both to be truthful. I may be . . . well no, there's a conflict there, yes. I've got ambivalent feelings about it. Sometimes I feel if only he'd go out and do the ordinary things that the other children do I'd feel so much better.

Cllr: Yes. But would he?

Catherine: Would *he*? [*pauses*] You know, sometimes he comes up to me and says 'Mum, I haven't got any friends', and then he'll just look at me, and I don't know what he . . . well, I don't quite know what.

Cllr: He may be asking if it's alright not to have friends amongst ordinary children who do ordinary things, do you think?

Catherine: Yes, I suppose he might be, I hadn't thought . . . yes . . . [*seems deep in thought*].

Cllr: Well, the reason I'm wondering that, Cathy, is that Paul has a lot of planets in fire signs. What we call fire signs in astrology have a basic quality of . . . well, it's a bit like this candle flame here [*points to a lighted candle in the room*]. I can't tell this flame where to go or what to do, it'll just flicker and dance its own routes, where it will, undirected and . . . [*interrupted*]

Catherine: Whew! . . . now that . . . Yes—you know I've offered him a lot of things lately: 'Would you like this, how about that' and he just slips by it all. Yes, I think you may have a point there. Maybe he's just trying to say 'Is it alright to dance my own routes'. He doesn't *want* to play football, or go swimming or cycling. I *can't* organize him. Oh Cathy you fool, and it's just because . . . [*pauses, takes a deep breath*] . . . it's because *I* don't feel comfortable—*I* don't feel comfortable!

From here the difference between the Earth and Fire signs was discussed a little more with Cathy, which led to the further conversation concerning Cathy's own Moon in Leo (a Fire sign) which she felt had been rather 'buried' in her life (see page 110).

7.
HOUSES AND ASPECTS

In 'event-oriented' astrology, the houses are designated as areas of specific experience and planets within each house are interpreted in terms of 'outcomes'. For example, Saturn in the second house is often translated as 'limitation of financial resources, impoverishment', which may well turn out to be so in a person's life, but in terms of self-development and understanding this kind of attempt at details is inappropriate and unhelpful. A flat interpretation like this gives a person the erroneous impression that he has no choice in the matter—that he is fated to be financially impoverished.

In astrological counselling, the counsellor will certainly bear in mind the tangible areas of activity denoted by the houses (home, marriage, money, children, career, etc.) but will also help the client understand the deeper principles underlying them. To some extent the houses parallel the meanings of the signs, but they reflect areas of life within which the processes and energies of signs are focused and will be further coloured by planets contained in the house.

Taking the same example of Saturn in the second house and its traditional interpretations of financial difficulty, when one considers that this placement appears in the chart of HRH the Prince of Wales (whose breadline existence is neither conspicuous nor discernible), we are led to the view that one's financial resources are but one manifestation of a quality within the individual himself at the second house stage of his chart. As will be seen from the house 'meanings' that follow, this particular house will have a bearing upon all of the resources the individual can bring to bear in his life—resources of stamina, courage (physical, moral, spiritual), creative resources, as well as material ones. All of these are ways in which he maintains his being and his standing, and thus renders himself secure after the initial thrusting energy of Aries/first house/Mars.

In this sense, the second house can be particularly pertinent in astrological counselling inasmuch as it can give a guide to the inner strengths available to the individual in times of difficulty and stress. The counsellor can draw on the principles of the sign on the 'cusp' (the starting point of the house), its Ruler, the planets in that house and their aspects, in order to help the client explore possible options and resources open to him to assist in coping and advancing through the stressful period. Quite often these may be what helped him through other, perhaps similar, crises earlier in his life—or it may be found that this area of the chart depicts ways in which the person may stay stuck in situations. For example, Saturn here may well be experienced by him from the standpoint of his vulnerability and be manifested via lack of or difficulty with material resources; or he may remain fixed in situations, however negative, since in

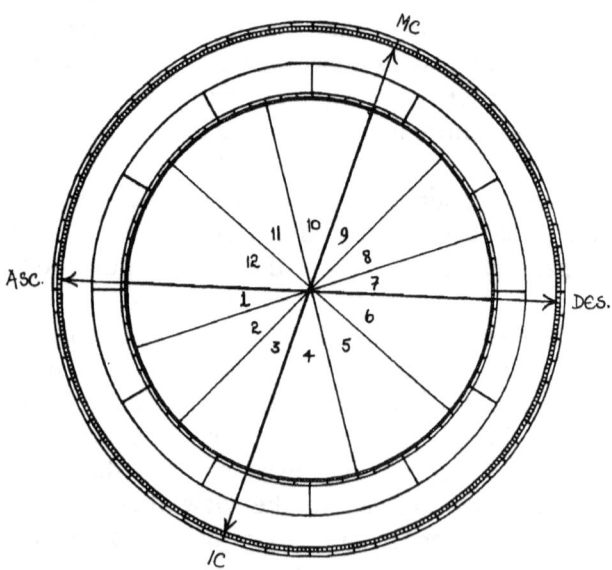

Figure 5. The Houses of the Chart.

their very bondage lies his sense of security. It is also, however, quite possible that the Saturnian principles of construct and responsibility will form the core inner resources that can enable him to maintain his ground with courage and integrity.

Most astrological textbooks will give clear descriptions of the different departments and activities of a person's life reflected by the houses. The following comments upon them reflect the inner processes which will also be borne in mind by the astrological counsellor. I should add that there are several systems of house division in astrology, all of which have relevance; with most astrologers it is a matter of choosing the one they feel works best and holds most relevance for themselves and their clients. The system shown in this book, and which is the one I use in practice, is the Placidus system, in which the Ascendant/Descendant and MC/IC respectively are the starting points for the first/seventh and tenth/fourth houses.

FIRST HOUSE
Reflecting the initiating energy of Aries, the action and drive of Mars.
♈ Asc. ♂

Starting point is the Ascendant; the individual's awareness of himself and personal impact upon his environment—both visual impact and via his semblance, mien, how he 'comes across'.

SECOND HOUSE
Reflecting the maintenance energy of Taurus and the values/desires of Venus.
♉ ♀

The individual's drive toward creating sustenance; acquiring that which has durability and stability, that which will perpetuate his security, lend him support; courage and other inner resources which enable him to maintain his ground.

THIRD HOUSE
Reflecting the mobility of Gemini, the communicative link of Mercury
♊ ☿

Emergence of intercommunication; the individual's understanding of and with his environment; how he moves among others and links his experiences, abilities, and thoughts with what he perceives around him.

FOURTH HOUSE
Reflecting the inner sense of belonging in Cancer, the private person at the IC, the habitual and familiar responses of the Moon.
♋ IC ☽

The cusp of this house is the IC. Personal integration, that which lends an inner sense of emotional security and familiarity; what instinctively binds the individual; his point of recoil, where he 'touches base' for emotional support; input of upbringing by parents in development of these values.

FIFTH HOUSE
Reflecting the self-display of Leo and the central path of purpose of the Sun's life-sustaining energy.
♌ ☉

Individual's capacity for personal display; what he feels good at and seeks to 'put up in lights', that which is potentially creative and fulfilling to his existence as a whole; power and supremacy in his self-expression.

SIXTH HOUSE
Reflecting the discrimination of Virgo, the understanding and awareness of Mercury
♍ ☿

Capacity for self-improvement through self-discrimination; psychological growth through self-examination; scanning over past experience; analysis of personal efficiency; where the individual seeks to purify something in himself by submitting self to channels through which he can learn and achieve order, synthesis, skill.

SEVENTH HOUSE
Reflecting the need for co-operation in Libra, the affectional drive of Venus.
♎ Desc. ♀

Starting point is the Descendant; the individual's awareness of others and participation with them (as opposed to first house awareness and establishment of himself); merging into social alliance, one-to-one relationships, that which the person seeks through human relatedness.

EIGHTH HOUSE
Reflecting the intense committment of Scorpio and the depth of Pluto.

♏ ♇

Deeper identification with others; intensification of relating, deeper committment and 'possession' of relationship (as opposed to acquisition of personal resources in the second house); where the individual earnestly searches below surface levels, where he seeks to lay 'depth charges' which open him to turning points of realization.

NINTH HOUSE
Reflecting the exploration of Sagittarius, the expansion of Jupiter.

♐ ♃

The individual's search for meaning, via finely attuned perceptions, philosophies; development of intuitions and wider beliefs (as opposed to perception of immediate environment in the third house); exploration of relationship between himself and the wider world; where the individual searches for profundity and breadth of vision.

TENTH HOUSE
Reflecting the social responsibility of Capricorn, the construct and clarification of Saturn.

♑ MC ♄

Starting point is the Midheaven; the public person and his goals; what the individual strives for and holds in esteem for himself; social identity through responsibility, direction, that which is prestigious and which he may uphold and lend weight to in the outer world (as opposed to that which constitutes emotional security in the fourth house); input of parental social values internalized through upbringing.

ELEVENTH HOUSE
Reflecting the progress/innovation of Aquarius, the breakthrough of Uranus.
♒ ♅

Where the individual can be socially creative (as opposed to personally creative in the fifth house); fulfilment of social goals in community at large and concern for amelioration of his wider group/society/ultimately the Universe via innovative contribution.

TWELFTH HOUSE
Reflecting the receptivity of Pisces, the inclusive energies of Neptune.
♓ ♆

Where the developing individual's energies are dissolved to merge with the greater Whole (as opposed to sixth house where his energies are directed toward personal review); withdrawal to unseen world; universality; unconscious energy developed in the course of time; that which is in the process of gestation, awaiting its fullness of time until externalization in . . .

FIRST HOUSE   The cycle of houses begins anew.

Aspects between planets and/or other points in the birth chart represent specific angular distances between them—60° between them is a sextile aspect, 90° a square, 120° a trine, 180° an opposition, and so on. Again, they can be read about in any book on the basic principles of astrology and are traditionally designated as 'easy' or 'difficult'. The symbols for the main aspects are written as follows:

Aspect	*Symbol*	*Orbs*	*Exact Aspect*
Conjunction	☌	0°—8°	0°
Semi-sextile	⌄	28°—32°	30°
Semi-square	∠	43°—47°	45°
Sextile	*	54°—66°	60°
Square	□	82°—98°	90°
Trine	△	112°—128°	120°
Sesquiquadrate	⚼	133°—137°	135°
Quincunx	⚻	148°—152°	150°
Opposition	☍	172°—180°	180°

In working with people, however, the astrological counsellor makes no rigid judgment as to whether an aspect is negative or otherwise in her client's life, but will know that at base the drives associated with the planets involved will be linked in *some* way within his nature (see Chapter 3, Part I). She is guided to the *quality of expression* needed for the aspect to operate by the *type* of aspect it is: traditionally 'difficult' aspects (squares, oppositions, etc.) are those which require action, will and purpose, or crisis, blockage and conflict in order for the person to build up endurance, strength and experience; this in turn increases his capacity for learning and psychological growth. The knocks and obstacles we encounter in our lives are potentially constructive processes and these aspects can therefore denote stalwart and creditable qualities which the individual is capable of developing.

Traditionally, 'easy' aspects (e.g. sextiles, trines) are those which do not usually require as much active input in the person's life but denote a blending or synthesis of planetary energies that enable him to expand his awareness, understanding, capacity for clarification and growth to greater maturity through fulfilment of tasks, creative ability, talents, skills—overall, a rather more effortless 'inner flow'. Nevertheless, this does not mean that these aspects are always automatically available for the individual to use; since they are more passive in quality, they may frequently need the active quality of, say, an adjoining square aspect to enable them to be put into operation.

Behind every aspect (as with everything in the birth chart) stands the individual himself. His outlooks, philosophies, conditioning and experiences so far in his life will all bear upon the way the aspect functions; it is he who lives it, or is seeking to live it, and his *actual* experience may not read exactly like a textbook interpretation.

Robert was born with Mercury (☿) in opposition to Saturn (♄) and both these planets were in square aspect to Mars (♂) in the fifth house. This is called a T-square in astrology and symbolizes a driving, dynamic quality in a person's life, although before such energy can be fully utilized it is often the case that the person can first experience it as strenuous and tense. Therein lies the will to construct. Often it denotes a struggle between the planetary energies drawn into the T-square, but one through which the person may well develop the capacity resolutely to fight, and thereby release the positive dynamics, to uncover the value and purpose held within the aspect pattern.

The counsellor has been explaining the principles of ☿ and ♄ (as mentioned on pp. 23-24) and now brings into the conversation the placement of ♂, explaining that this represents action/energy directed into areas of life where the client can be creative, reach fulfilment, enjoyment, play, 'shine', be 'a winner' (fifth house). Robert is a very successful and prolific playwright and journalist, which seems to fit the principles of this T-square very well, although the struggle a T-square can normally bring is not clear in the light of Robert's apparently easy use of his creative talent and his success. However, the counsellor continues the conversation on this, since she notes a transit of ♀ to the natal ☿ (which would trigger the whole T-square). This introduces a current need for some kind of disintegration or stripping away of the qualities contained within it, so that a powerful transformation can take place, or something hidden deep within needs now to be brought to light which could turn Robert around into a new phase of his life:

Robert: The thing I was wondering whether the chart could help me with is that . . . well, maybe it's this Mercury/Saturn you mentioned . . . but the thing is, I'm going through the most *gynormous* writing block at the moment. I just can't seem to . . . well, you should've heard me being interviewed on the radio the other night . . . God, it was awful [*shakes head sadly*].

Cllr: [*Thinking this sounds very like Pluto whose process of crumbling, disintegration, leading to a new cycle can often be initially felt as a huge block*] Really—what happened?

Robert: Dried up, didn't I? I felt *so* nervous . . . somehow when it comes to talking . . . I don't know . . . my voice was getting fainter and fainter . . . terrifying!

Cllr: Yes, it must have been . . . I find talking with you very easy, but do you feel terrified . . . [*interrupted*]

Robert:	Oh *no*—no, it's not like here, us just talking here—this is fine, but those suave interviewers firing their questions and . . . oh, I don't know, I felt like a small kid somehow.
Cllr:	So the writing block is also a speaking block?
Robert:	Yes. Well, that's what it felt like the other night.
Cllr:	Yes, I've only ever done that—radio interviews I mean —a few times, and I didn't like it much either, but did you ever feel like that when you were an *actual* kid . . . I mean, what happened if you expressed an opinion . . . [*focusing into Mercury/Saturn as a way of discerning whether Saturn as an internalized 'authority figure' (via a parent perhaps) was repressive to Robert's Mercurial communication of ideas, thoughts*].
Robert:	Oh God, the old man would have my hide . . . unless, of course, I said anything he absolutely agreed with.
Cllr:	[*Bearing in mind that Robert has ☽ square to ♅ and ♂ in ♒ which suggest a good deal of individuality in Robert's make-up—one which would not readily 'tow the line'.*] Was that very often? [*smiles a little*].
Robert:	Frankly, no [*smiles back*] . . . I was always saying something radically different . . . a bit of a rebel, I suppose.
Cllr:	How did he have your hide? Did he hit you?
Robert:	No, not really—he'd just bawl me out . . . stand up and yell at me to get out.
Cllr:	[*Probing a little further in order to help Robert follow through and connect with the experience perhaps a little more than he has previously done*] What happened then?
Robert:	Well, I guess everyone would just make a joke of it . . . cheer me up sort of thing—they'd say things like 'What, old man blown 'is top again 'as 'e . . . never mind!' . . . and tousle my hair, things like that.
Cllr:	And what were you feeling?

Robert: ★★★ mad! [*Grits teeth*].

Cllr: Yes, it must have been pretty hurtful too.

Robert: Yup! So I didn't do it too often . . . hardly made a murmur most of the time.

Cllr: So none of it really got expressed and dealt with . . . by people trying to cheer you up, which was them being kind and showing concern perhaps? [*Robert nods*] . . . by snapping you out of it, you never got to express the anger and hurt . . . and possibly the humiliation? . . . . except of course you have channelled it creatively through your writing [*Robert's plays contain many themes of people in families fighting in desperation to express themselves. From what Robert has said we can also gain a glimpse of the T-square type of struggle, which eventually releases positive dynamics*] . . . but somehow when questions are fired at you in a radio interview . . .

Robert: [*Staring straight ahead of him*] Yes, I'd never realized how . . . I guess . . . well, there must be a lot of those feelings still all sitting there.

The T-square, being transited by Pluto (♀) and manifesting as a block, seems to be heralding the time for release and elimination of all that is pent-up in it, still 'all sitting there' and physically manifested in the gritted teeth as Robert recalls his early experiences of tense oppression of his originality and 'rebel' ideas. It is highly likely that in Robert's psyche the radio interviewers took on the image of this oppressive authority ('firing their questions'), pitching Robert back into responding as he had earlier in his life—'hardly making a murmur', 'dried up', 'getting fainter and fainter'. The clarification he has reached enables him to progress into the area of tension and start to release the trapped energy (the 'block') by getting in touch with the residual feelings, and this was to form part of his later work in psychotherapy. When we have been through periods where people have 'snapped us out of' our feelings, there can come a time when we need to snap back into them again so that we can clear them and then move on.

HOUSES AND ASPECTS

★ ★ ★ ★ ★

Maureen is a secretary who is good at her work and enjoys it, but she mentioned during a discussion of her chart that she was having difficulty concentrating on her work at the moment because of emotional upsets she was having with her husband. Maureen has the Sun (☉) in Gemini (♊) in the third house and she readily agreed that what she most enjoys about her job is having many contacts with her boss's clients, arranging meetings, conferences, etc. (☉♊ third house), and she gets on very well with the other people she works with. But when it comes to focusing on her twelfth house Moon (☽) in Pisces (♓) (where her feelings are oceanic in their depth) she says:

Maureen: Sometimes I get to feeling very closed off . . . people wonder what's going on . . . I just go inside somehow . . . feeling very intense. Sometimes I feel so . . .

Cllr: Is it that you're feeling something so intensely that you're overcome?

Maureen: Yes, sort of. You see, I can appear quite OK—I mean I get on with the job and keep things running smoothly, you know . . . I mean I like to keep busy, like you were saying about Gemini, but, well, underneath . . . well, I feel very shaky sometimes . . . there's so much . . . I mean, if I let it all out I . . . er . . . oh!

Cllr: I sometimes have something similar going on in me— with me it's a sort of [*tries to find a Water analogy for Maureen's* ☽ ♓] well, a bit like a duck all busily swimming smooth and unruffled on the top and . . .

Maureen: Yes!—and paddling like mad underneath! [*both laugh*] Yes, that's pretty much how it is for me.

Cllr: [*Talks a little more about the depth of* ☽ *in* ♓ *in the twelfth house, its sensitivity, its impressionability and how, generally speaking, people with this placement of the* ☽ *are frequently open and receptive to every subtlety, every nuance in the environment which they readily soak up and add to their already fathomless*

92 ASTROLOGICAL COUNSELLING

emotions] If you let them all out you said? Are you worried that they might engulf you or that they'll overwhelm everyone else?

Maureen: Both. Yes, both. Yes it *is* like that... it's, well it's like I'm tossed around in one emotion after another and then I can't concentrate on work [*the ☽ is in square aspect to ☉ in ♊, hence the experience of conflict in these two areas of Maureen's life*] ... but mainly it's ... well, maybe that's why . . . Keith [*her husband*] complains that I just clam up you see . . . hmm, twelfth house . . . yes, it all churns around kind of underground and I don't . . .

Cllr: Do you clam up to save *him* from being overwhelmed do you think?

★ ★ ★ ★ ★

Mrs M. with Sun (☉) conjunct Pluto (♇) in Gemini (♊), Mercury (☿) conjunct Mars (♂) and opposition Uranus (♅), also square to Saturn (♄). At the time this conversation took place, Mrs M. was seventy and just beginning to take an interest in astrology. A discussion of ☿ conjunct ♂ and opposition ♅ was under way along the lines of its potential for astuteness, quick perception, flair for equally quick comprehension and much depth of thought (with ♄):

Mrs M: Yes, using my mind in quick-witted ways has always been important to me, but do you know I can say that all through my life people have not taken me as being as intelligent as I really am. And when I do say something that's intelligent, they're really surprised. I found this when I was nursing [*Mrs M. was a Nursing Sister for many years*] . . . somehow no one expected me to quite understand, or they felt they had to spell things out and show me how.

Cllr: And all the time you knew anyway!

Mrs M: Yes! And when it became apparent that I not only knew already but also knew more than they did, they were really surprised!

Cllr: They?

Mrs M: Oh, I mean doctors, people like that.

Cllr: I see—and how did you feel about them? It must have been irritating to . . . [*interrupted; endeavouring to focus on ☉ conjunct ♀ and the squares to ♄ with their possible need for control*].

Mrs M: Oh, some of them were hopeless . . . you had to watch your place mind you, but many's the time I wanted to say 'Oh give it here, let me do it'.

Cllr: Yes, I suppose when you can see things very quickly and you've mastered them it must be very easy to feel you want to take over.

Mrs M: Well, not just that, but if you've got a sick patient lying there on the other end of their dithering . . . [*the counsellor is brought to a sharp reminder of Mrs M's Virgo Ascendant with its theme of concern for the welfare of others*].

Cllr: Yes, yes I see. Nursing must have meant a great deal to you [*Probably trying to make up for overlooking ♍ by focusing on it!*]

Mrs M: Well, it was just that most of us girls went into nursing. It was usually the done thing, but there might have been other . . . well, I might have liked to teach, or maybe languages [*Asc. ♍, ☉ ♊, ☽ third ♐ in Mrs M's chart are now discussed with her, since these all hold potential for the careers Mrs M. might alternatively have pursued. When the counsellor described the process of ☽ in ♐, Mrs M. also added that she would have liked to have travelled in her life and at one time had wanted very much to emigrate to New Zealand*].

Cllr: So in the end you plumped for nursing because it was the usual thing? Did you ever talk over these other possibilities—I mean with your family, parents? [*Scanning the usual chart significators of parents, ☉ conjunct ♀ in the tenth, ♄ in the eighth square to ☿ and ♂, ☽ in wide opposition to the ☉*].

Mrs M: Didn't talk to my parents much at all. They were both Aquarians, you know. They're supposed to be very remote aren't they?

Cllr: Well, that can be one way of people using Aquarius— were your parents remote then?

Mrs M: Well, Mother... she was stern. She mellowed a lot in her later years, but she was stern. And Father, well... [*a long pause: if one takes the ☉ and ♄ as significators of one's father, the ☉ is ☌ ♇ and ♄ occupies the eighth house; thus there is a strong focus on a possible theme of difficulty in deeply committed relationship (♇, ♏ and eighth house), isolation and emotional pain generally associated with the father, and which Mrs M's long pause may well be bringing to mind. She continues...*] ... well, I really didn't know him too well. When I was a child you see he worked in the town all the time and we were miles away in the village, so he was only ever home occasionally—and then I went away to school, and then I was nursing... so you see I only ever saw him once in a blue moon and [*pause*] well, I've never said this to anyone before, but, well, to tell you the truth... I really didn't like him... no, I really didn't like him much at all.

★ ★ ★ ★ ★

Pamela has been married once, but it only lasted a matter of a year or so because her husband drank a lot and ran around after many other women. Pam describes him as a no-good who got entangled in all kinds of impossible schemes and escapades about which they had many stormy arguments. She adds that he made her feel very worthless and depressed.

The Sun (☉) and Mars (♂) in a woman's chart are taken as significators of the type of masculine spirit she looks for and attracts in her relationships with men. Here, they are conjunct in Pisces (♓) and ♂ is within orb of a quincunx (150°) aspect to Neptune (♆) on the eighth house cusp (♆ the ruler of Pisces). This suggests the type of 'lightweight' martian energy which Pam seems to have met through this relationship, i.e. one that is unfocused, emotion-

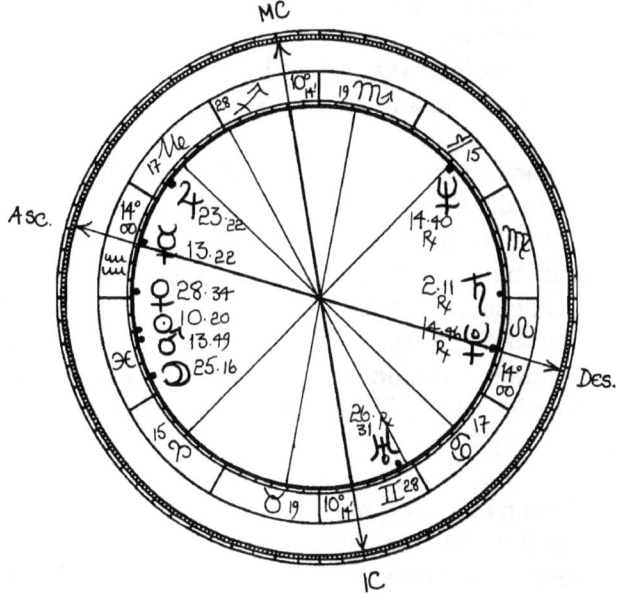

Figure 6. Pamela's Chart.

ally muddled, entangled in foggy webs rather than clearly directed. They are in wide opposition to Saturn (♄) in the seventh house, there is a closer opposition of Venus (♀) and ♄, and Pluto (♇) falls on the Descendant. Together these highlight the 'worthless and depressed' feelings attributed to her partner's behaviour, as well as the powerful and destructive 'stormy arguments' they went through.

Pam is a very dynamic, artistic and original person who has lived her life in exciting and adventurous ways (Asc. ♒, ☽ □ ♅, ☉ ☽ ♓, MC ♐). She is a talented painter and designs her own clothes; but more than anything else she has enjoyed travelling the world (♐ MC, ☿ rising) and to this end has worked as a courier and in travel firms. Having ended her first marriage, Pam then met Tony who has ☉ ☌ ♄ in ♍ (☍ her ☉ ♂). Tony has ♐ on the Ascendant and shares with Pam a love of travelling. When they met he was also working as a courier/travel guide and eventually they decided to start a venture of their own in travel and tour services. Pam put a great deal of flair and energy (♒, ☽ □ ♅, ☉ ☌ ♂) alongside Tony's organizational skills (☉ ☌ ♄ in ♍); she was also instrumental in helping him make new contacts and had a knack of sensing the right things at the right time generally (♓, ☽ □ ♅ 4th, ♃ 12th). Amongst it all they fell in love and married. They both wanted to have a child and were delighted when Michelle, their baby daughter, was born.

However, Pam began to feel very distraught because Tony was working practically all the time keeping the travel service going; occasionally he travelled abroad, but he was also out most evenings working in the bureau organizing tour programmes or otherwise meeting other people and contacts. All in all, Pam saw very little of him. As Pam and the counsellor talk, Pam's distress seems to contain some muddled emotion (♓, ♆ 8th) dramatic fury and a few verbal histrionics (☽ □ ♅ 4th, ♓, ☿ ☍ ♀ across Asc./Desc. ♒/♌):

Pam: I mean that ★ ★ ★ man is out five nights a week at *least*! I can't stand it much longer. Sometimes I think I shall just ★ ★ ★ leave and that's all there is to it [*powerful ultimatums from* ☉ ☌ ♂, ☿ ☍ ♀, ♒/♌].

Cllr: You're thinking of leaving Tony altogether?

Pam: Well, I am *not* going to go on like this much longer that's for sure [*furious and adamant*].

Cllr: Yes, if he's away most evenings that must be pretty grim, especially if you're left alone with the baby [*pauses*]. How many evenings would you like Tony to be home?

Pam: Well, at least three or four, I mean that's not too much to ★ ★ ★ ask surely!

Cllr: No, I wouldn't have thought so [*pauses*]. I can understand that you're feeling angry and upset Pam, but at the same time I have the feeling that in the process your needs are getting a bit muddled up. You see, if Tony's out five evenings a week and you'd like him home three or four, I don't quite see how leaving him is going to get you nearer . . . I mean, by leaving you'd have him with you *no* evenings a week.

Pam: [*Big sigh*] OK, but what else can I do to make him *see*?!

Cllr: Hmm. [*Pause*] Are you banking on the fact that by creating a storm and marching out on him he'd then come running after you and beg you to stay? [*The dramatic gestures of* ☽ ☐ ♅, ☿ ☍ ♀, ☊ / ♒ *which, perhaps to avoid the inner vulnerability and aloneness of* ♀ ☍ ♄ 7th, *could be Pam's pattern of having relationships fail*].

Pam: N... [*Sighs*] Well, yes, I suppose I am [*sighs again and is quieter*].

Cllr: [*Quietly*] So what if he doesn't?

Pam: I don't know... I just don't know... I don't know what else... I mean, I've tried talking to him, but it's no good. Oh, they're all the same... I mean he spends all the time at the ★★★ bureau, but it was *me* who helped him get all that together, it was *me* who did most of the work. He *couldn't* have done it on his own. Oh, these ★★★ men, they marry you, you have their kids and then they swan off and do their own thing.

Cllr: Like Richard? [*Pam's first husband*].

Pam: Yes, just like ★★★ Richard!

Cllr: [*Spends a little while explaining the themes of* ♀ ☍ ♄ *vulnerability, aloneness, expectations of burden/isolation and the* ☽ ☐ ♅, ♒ *need for freedom and excitement, which Pam sounds as if she's missing. She may resent this and also has an image of men as being incapable and unreliable* ♓/♆. *The counsellor asks Pam, more directly this time:*] Are you feeling trapped left at home with the baby?

Pam: [*Looks directly at the counsellor for the first time and answers quickly*] Yes.

Cllr: Yes, and I think that this is important and needs to be dealt with. In fact, it may be the first thing because it sounds like a lot of pressure may have built up there. It's tough being on your own with a small baby to look after, particularly after the kind of dynamic life you were living [*trying to elicit how much a sense of loss there may be*]...

Pam: [*Head in hands*] Oh, I *do* miss it Christina . . . I miss it [*begins to cry*].

Cllr: Yes [*remains quiet while Pam cries*].

Once Pam's distress has abated, she and the counsellor go over again some of the earlier factors they covered in the chart concerning Pam's need for freedom, her beliefs about men and her expectations of being trapped and depressed by them, as well as Tony's potentially competent and responsible ☉ ☌ ♄ in ♍, her own volcanic tirades, loneliness, resentment and whether or not she enjoys being a mother. By the end of the session, the counsellor is therefore able to draw several threads of their discussion together, which can then be used as a basis for further work:

Cllr: So there are really three main things we've come to—first, there's your own role as a supportive, caring woman and mother, but also the more assertive spirit within you which also claims to be lived. There's also the fact that, yes, you have given Tony a lot of help and it's possible that he may feel responsible because of that and work doubly hard to keep it all going. But, alongside, are your feelings that all men are useless and incapable, which, while intact, you may always find will put you in situations where you feel let down, or hurt, or trapped? [*Pam nods*] Well I'm wondering whether these expectations are also something Tony picks up [*his* ☉ ♄ ☍ *her* ☉ ♂], so again he works hard to prove himself and maybe stays away from home to avoid . . . well . . .

Pam: [*With a smile*] Go on, you might as well say it—I nag! [*both laugh*].

Cllr: Well, actually what was going through my mind just then was that the whole question of competence or otherwise might also be a personal one for Tony. It's very likely that he is a very responsible and able person and stays away from home, working hard, to avoid being deflected from that, but it might also be to avoid the whole issue of why he personally holds so much investment in that ... but that's pure hypothesis on my part, based only on a sort of general pattern I've seen with Virgo, which usually *abhors* incompetence and wants to go 'somewhere' rather than 'nowhere'. But we'd really have to hear Tony to see what relevance this might have for him.

Pam: Yes, I see. Actually it's true, I do see most men as incompetent, but Tony isn't quite like that.

Cllr: And then of course there's Michelle, who [*interrupted*].

Pam: Yes, well ... I do miss working but I'm sure I'd miss her if I just went straight back into taking an active part. Actually, if the truth be known I'd feel guilty. I can't help feeling trapped.

Cllr: Perhaps the 'trapped' feeling would be a good place to start. Tell me, do you tend to go about things all-independently ... 'I'll go it alone' sort of thing? (♒, ☽ □ ♅, ☉ ☌ ♄) or, well, what I'm really trying to ask is, how easy would it be for you to ask for help from ... [*interrupted*].

Pam: Oh yes, I've been thinking while we've been talking ... yes, you're right, I do tend to go it alone, but if I could get a little help with Michelle and the house, well I think that would make it easier for me ... I'd have more time to concentrate on Tony and me and where it's all heading.

Pam was able to arrange some regular help in looking after the baby so that she could have more time and space to sort out the difficulties in her relationship with Tony and in counselling work continued to explore the patterns she has been living. She was eventually able to talk about these from the basis of the chart to Tony, who became very interested in exploring his own chart, so they were able to re-establish lines of communication. Later on, they worked together with a Marriage Guidance Counsellor on the issues their astrological charts had principally brought to light and began to learn astrology themselves as an adjunct to helping them clarify their situation.

8.
KEY POINTS: PROGRESSIONS, TRANSITS, AND MAJOR CYCLES

If the birth chart is regarded as a guide to the tapestry of a person's life (with that person as the weaver), these key points depict the threads which are required next to be interwoven as he moves through different stages of his life. Thus, each colour, each texture of the basic overall pattern is incorporated into the framework. They are neither indicators nor causes of precise events, but refer to phases of our growth which unfold in the sequence of time and which are regarded in the light of the initial pattern of energies and potentialities, as represented by the natal chart.

The progression of a birth chart entails taking each succeeding day after birth as representative of the appropriate succeeding year of life (the second day represents the second year, the twentieth day the twentieth year, and so on). The progressed planetary positions are then related both to each other and to the natal chart.

Of course, everyone knows that astrology has a popular, if mistaken, reputation as a doctrine of fated events which can be foretold, but this outlook is far removed from the work of the present-day astrological counsellor. It is hardly conducive to an individual's well-being, increased self-understanding and opportunities for psychological growth to deliver specific announcements of events to befall him (even if this were possible) coupled with homely advice on how best to avoid the dire and dreadful or incitements to make hay on the good days. But old archaic images die hard and it can often fall to the modern-day astrologer to explain the truer significance of progressions to her clients, as indeed it does to help the client who may have consulted the type of practitioner whose set predictions have sparked off inner fear, worry and distress.

As we have seen earlier, neither the human being nor his universe are motionless. Together they form one gigantic living and progressive alliance, forever on the move even though periods of tranquillity, stagnation and inertia are encountered. Because we are in a two-way dance with our universe, we need to co-operate with it and learn our 'steps'. Many astrologers dispatch the message that by looking at the future condition of the heavens 'forewarned is forearmed', but it seems to me that this choice of wording only serves to escalate deeply-held fears that there is something only negative and hostile 'out there' that we need to be 'warned' and 'armed' against. Moreover, it perpetrates the notion of a chasm between the cosmos and man and infers that we must live splintered off from that which is around us. Particularly at this stage of our evolution, when we live in a world so beset with splits and dissensions of many kinds, it seems to me that if we can put as much energy into being *for* our cosmos as we have into being against it, we may then go a long way to healing these clefts on Earth and living in a world of less fragmentation.

The astrological counsellor is not a predictor of events but, together with her client, is a translator of the tapestry and the nature of the threads to be interlaced next; exactly *how* they are interlaced and what that piece of the tapestry turns out to be must be the client's choice—the counsellor is there to talk over the nature and options of the progression that can enable that choice to be clarified and reached.

The progressed, transiting and cyclic motions of a birth chart may well manifest in tangible and concrete events if that is the avenue along which the person opens himself to the meaning of each key point. It is just as likely that their manifestation can emerge through changes of outlook, behaviour, feelings, thoughts, attitudes, awarenesses, etc., ranging all the way from the subtle to the overt. Indeed there is no distinction between 'event' and 'change of attitude' when one considers that outer occurrences reflect our inner lives, and vice versa. Sometimes we become so stultified in our past and present that we fail to open ourselves to look at the meaning of what we should be doing or being. Then we may become mere collectors of events, some of which we might well consider we could do without; but a closer examination reveals that whatever has transpired has been the result of our own choice. We cannot then insist it is all the fault of our stars.

Sometimes, events occur in our lives over which we seem to have no control, which appear as bolts from the blue slicing a way through our lives. Often these can be events of deep tragedy and it is understandably hard for the human being to attune himself to anything else other than crying out in anguish, shock and pain. Few people in this situation are going to be immediately open to looking at deeper meanings, still less to considering that the crisis could be harnessed to anything in themselves. In such circumstances intellectual, astrological (or any other) considerations and explanations would be misplaced in taking precedence over the human need to move fully into those feelings—to grieve, to rage, to mourn and cry. If this does not occur, that grief and anger can often become trapped and stored inside, only to re-emerge in some other form—as physical complaints for instance (such as ulcers or intestinal spasms) or yet another event through which the psyche attempts to relieve pressure. It is often at key periods of life when there is such a crisis, or some kind of momentous event which brings despair and pain, that the astrological counsellor, who has insight into the nature of the process from the planetary principles involved in that experience, can help the person find channels amongst the multitudinous psychotherapies and counselling approaches available today (e.g. Gestalt, Psychodrama, Transactional Analysis, Bioenergetics, Psychosynthesis, Creative Journal Work and many other modern systems of both 'depth' and 'height' psychology. The reader is referred to further sources of information concerning these in Appendix II).

Through acknowledging and working with our individual growth process, we can allow all that it contains—events, feelings, changes, etc.—to flow, rather than get trapped inside us again. Through astrology, the person can gradually understand that the circumstances we meet in our lives are those with which our nature has a particular affinity. By working with the heavens and making conscious steps to understand the parallels between their movements and the tides of our lives, we may have less need for chaos, confusion and catapulting events; instead we can gain enlightenment as to what is involved and what we may need to do. Often progressions and transits over focal points in a chart during a lifetime will point up a series of connected experiences which are like messages flashed to the person as to the themes to be sorted out and incorporated. This was partly the case with Thelma (page 112) and conversations with the astrological counsellor can help the client decipher what needs to be done, where the work to personal growth and change lies.

Whereas a *progression* is the movement of a planet during the course of life from one point to another, following the symbolic path of a day for a year, a *transit* is the passage of a planet in the heavens at the current time over a planetary position at birth. Thus, at the time of writing this, Pluto in the sky occupies 26° of Libra and if this forms any aspect to other points in my own birth chart, I would say I was experiencing a Pluto transit. Such transits arouse the themes associated with the planets involved. They are looked at in the light of the basic chart pattern and its development via other progressed and transiting factors that have occurred and are occurring in the person's life. *Cycles* in the chart refer to specific periods of life, concurrent with age development and common to every person, when planets (particularly the outer planets) reach significant positions in relation to each other and to their birth placement. Overall, they mark important transitions from youth to old age and the varying levels of development contained within each stage.

Marjorie has been married for very many years to Neil. She telephones to say that she is trying to sort out things in her mind since she is wondering where their marriage is heading; also, in her life generally, she feels some kind of transition is going on but is unable to pinpoint what it is about. Marjorie does not live in England and, where she is, there is no one she can consult. However, she is due to make a flying visit to London and feels it might help her if she can spend some time talking things over with the astrological counsellor.

There are three progressions of planets into new signs—the Sun (☉), Mercury (☿) and Venus (♀). Planets progress through a sign for many years but at the point of entry there is usually an especial theme to be lived concerning the nature of both planet and sign. Progressed ☉ and ☿ have entered Scorpio (♏). Pluto (♇ the ruler of ♏) is transiting the IC, having recently completed a transit by trine to the Moon (☽) in the eighth house (the natural house of ♇ and ♏). Thus there is a focus upon the need for deeper discovery of oneself, perhaps more particularly one's emotional self (☽ 8th) with the accompanying theme of transforming, stripping away, bringing to awareness that which has lain unexamined and unexplored. Insofar as Marjorie has voiced the feeling of a 'transition', Pluto transiting the fourth house cusp (IC) frequently accompanies some kind of upheaval on the home/domestic front, but at a deeper level it marks the need for an upheaval of inner emotional patterns which she may have grown used to. Something in this area of her life may need to be torn down and reconstructed in a new and better way, or at least given a thorough 'spring clean'.

As well as transiting the IC of course, ♇ may well serve to open up the opposite point, the MC which is Aries (♈). The ruler of the MC, Mars (♂), forms a T-square with ☉ and Saturn (♄). This suggests a great deal of endurance, stamina, capability and

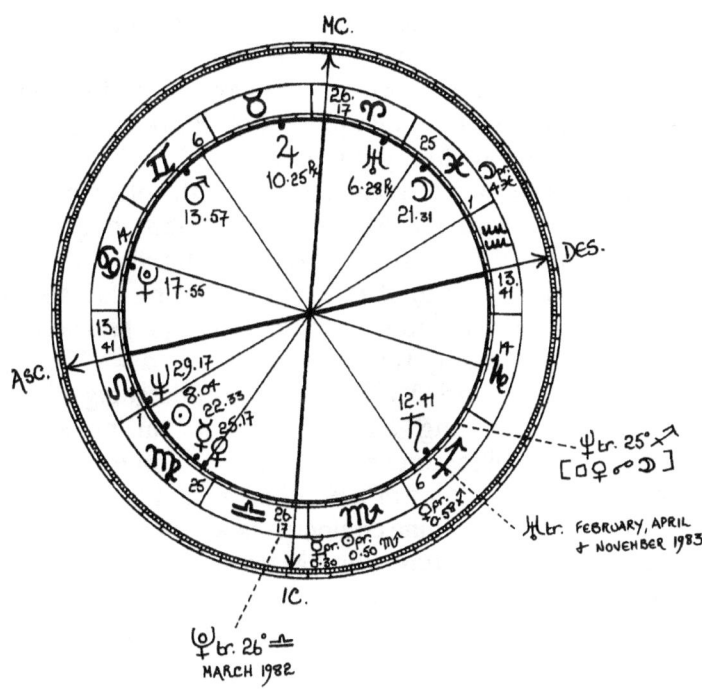

Figure 7. Marjorie's Chart.

practicality to Marjorie's nature on the one hand, but these may also have been experienced through fighting oppression, a lack of freedom in her life, or the feeling of being constrained by obligations. Jupiter (♃) in the tenth house, the natural house of ♄ and Capricorn (♑) may similarly be manifested as a strong sense of duty. If these aspects of the chart have been experienced negatively, Marjorie's full expression of ♈ MC's potential for self-assertion in her pursuit of individual goals may somehow be blocked; so this too may constitute part of the discussion when the astrological counsellor meets her.

Venus (♀) progressed has now moved into Sagittarius (♐), strengthening the focus on the need for greater freedom, a wide berth or breathing space. In the past year, ♀ will have squared, by progression, the natal Neptune (♆). In the birth chart, ♀ is in ♍, ☍ ☽ ♓; the ☽ ruler is Neptune (♆), which is unaspected in the first house and, at the time of consultation, the progressed ☽ is in opposition to the ☉/♆ midpoint (halfway between ☉ and ♆). The natal aspects suggest a great deal of caring sympathy and sensitivity to Marjorie's nature and this is now highlighted by these progressions. Perhaps with the possible need for a breathing space mentioned above, Marjorie is endeavouring to free herself from areas of life in which the discipline of ☉/♂/♄ and ♍/♓ themes of service/sacrifice are brought into play.

There is also an additional theme of depth, intensity, passion and committment with the Moon in the eighth house, and Pluto (natural ruler of the eighth) in Cancer (♋), the Moon's natural sign. It is likely again that all this is being focused upon for adjustment and dissolution with the recent progression of ♀ □ ♆ and ♆ itself currently transiting both ☽ and ♀. The emotional metamorphosis which Marjorie may be undergoing most probably contains a 'slackening' (♆) of the emotional intensity she may have put into looking after others' needs (☽ 8th ♓) perhaps out of a sense of duty, discipline or a need for control (☉/♂/♄).

All of these are outline components which can become clarified as to their actual setting when Marjorie arrives. The counsellor might begin to interpret this, for instance (and as already intimated), along the lines of Marjorie perhaps using the ☽/♀/♓ ♍ (sympathetic/caring/wanting to help part of her nature), together with the tough/determined/or oppressive ☉/♂/♄ content as thorough competence and indispensability to others. With ♆ rising unaspected in the first house, perhaps there is again a strong drive toward over-helpfulness and a martyred feeling because of it. All of these things may now need to be relinquished in view of the ♆ and ♀ transits.

When Marjorie comes and puts the counsellor in the picture, she explains that a couple of years previously Neil had been made redundant. After spending a while sailing (his hobby), he took a job in the Caribbean. He was then offered another in Florida, where he now is and has been for several months. Marjorie's elderly mother has been living with them for the past four years (since ☉ progressed crossed the IC), which Marjorie initially felt happy about, but she is now finding it a strain, particularly with Neil away so much. She has a good job as Director of an accountancy firm, but the responsibility of that, coupled with 'undiluted Mum' is again felt as a strain. Now the question has arisen as to whether she should join Neil in Florida, what she can possibly do about her mother if she does, also what she should do about her own job (can she, would she really want to, give it up?). Amongst it all is the dilemma of whether she should live her life caring, yielding, giving to other people (i.e. Neil and/or her mother), or whether she should start to build up her own career, which is currently offering her more scope. But then what happens to the marriage? All of this is accompanied by much guilt and fear of being considered selfish.

The outlines the counsellor has scanned over in the chart are thus thrown into relief. It is unlikely that they can all be dealt with in one session but together Marjorie and the counsellor begin to sort out possible options which are open to her concerning the four issues of Neil, her mother, her job and her home, since this is what Marjorie most asked for when she telephoned.

When it comes to discussing her work, and the counsellor explains ♈ MC and ♀ now transiting in opposition, Marjorie says she feels there *is* something she still would like to pursue and achieve for herself. Because her job is now offering more scope in many directions she would like greater freedom to follow these. But she does feel under a lot of constraint, both from Neil being away so much and wanting her to join him in Florida, and her elderly mother who 'sits like a queen being looked after'. There is also the constraint of her own 'internal supervisor', who says this is what she should be, ought to be, doing/suffering (the T-square).

There is a form of psychotherapy called Transactional Analysis, which postulates the theory of a 'life script'—a model or design for our lives (like the script of a play) which each of us formulates during childhood. Marjorie's script may run along the lines of 'Unflinching Duty in Rendering Service to Others', a pattern often sustained by feelings of obligation and guilt and which, again, may well be what Marjorie is endeavouring to review.

However, beneath it all are Marjorie's deeper feelings concerning Neil and she begins to voice expectations that the marriage may end. The counsellor endeavours to steer the conversation to a point where the ☽ ♀/♍ ♓/♆ elements of the chart might receive greater personal clarification for Marjorie without the counsellor forcing her own interpretations upon her. In turn, this might help Marjorie draw nearer to analysing whether or not the marriage does in fact need to end, or whether it is just some aspect of it which requires adjustment (♀ prog. just passed natal ♆, and ♆ tr. ☽ and ♀)—such as, again, Marjorie's possible part in inviting the constraints by being thoroughly helpful and indispensable. Additionally, if Marjorie wants more freedom to pursue her own goals, the ♅ transit in 1983 ☌ ♄ will activate the whole ☉/♂/♄ T-square, signifying Marjorie's need to release (♅) herself from the constraints. It is therefore appropriate for her to be looking into the implications of this T-square now, so that by the time the ♅ transit is exact she will have done some initial groundwork; it is then less likely to take her by surprise through sudden disruptions. Finally, if Marjorie is feeling her own needs/goals are negated in her present way of life, is the whole question of recognition a main issue for Marjorie? (♄ is in the fifth house and ♌, the fifth sign, is on the Ascendant.) The counsellor asks Marjorie:

Cllr: What do you feel is the *main* difficulty between you and Neil, I mean in the relationship itself? How do you feel about . . .

Marjorie: Well now, I was thinking about that the other day. I had a letter from him, and there was a line in that which just about summed it up for me really. He was telling me all about the people and situations, you know, all the different things he was meeting out there, and then he said [*pulls letter out from her bag to read it*] 'I wish you were here to make it all come clear for me'. And I thought *THAT'S IT! That's* what I've always done. I'm always the one to make things clear, who takes care of things and sees him through them, and I feel *drained* by it and I feel drained by Mum. I'm always the one who ... [*Marjorie is experiencing for herself how she has used the main factors of her chart which the counsellor now puts into words for her:*]

Cllr: You're always the one who takes care of things for other people, everything is on your shoulders.

Marjorie: Yes, that's right—it's *always* been me ... [*pause*] but, you know, this is the first time, the *very first time*, that Neil has ever acknowledged that.

Cllr: [*Pause*] So, is your feeling of being drained *because* you've always taken care of, taken on all the burdens? [*pause*] ... or is it because you've never had any acknowledgement of it?

Marjorie: Ah! [*Long pause*] Good question [*pause*]. I'll have to think about that one.

After a pause again, the counsellor goes over the main components of the chart, which clarify for Marjorie the realizations of herself which she has just reached. The Ψ, $♀$ and forthcoming $⛢$ transits are also explained so that Marjorie can be aware that these patterns within her now need to be changed. This in turn validates Marjorie's initial feeling of a 'transition', which she had voiced when she first telephoned. The counsellor asks:

Cllr: Do you feel these are things you might be able to talk over with Neil?

Marjorie: I could try, but one of the things with him is that he never thinks a marriage is something you need to talk about, or work at. To him, it's something you just *do*. I mean you get married and that's it ... it's just there. He'll never talk about it or discuss things. I don't think he's got any idea that people grow and change at all or that anything needs discussion.

Cllr: Yes, that must be very frustrating, like a brick wall that's difficult to get through [*Marjorie's* ☉/♂/♄]. But [*in case Marjorie is wanting to shift the onus entirely on to Neil*] I'm wondering whether, with these transits we've talked about, plus the fact that Neil has made a small start to acknowledge you, whether that might be a starting point for you to break through some of these patterns of feeling held back and always giving, taking care of. Perhaps you could talk to him about that line he wrote and explain that you've become aware that you . . . [*interrupted*]

Marjorie: Oh yes, yes—he's coming home the weekend after next for a short while, I might be able to . . . The thing is, now that I *know*, well this has clarified a lot. I mean now that I know that what I felt to be going on *is* there to be dealt with, this transition . . . yes, now that I have that, well yes, I think I could have a chat with him and see where we go from there.

It is a pity that there is no one near Marjorie with whom she can start on some continued counselling, but she and the counsellor arrange for a written summary of the main themes of the birth chart to be sent to her, together with the current progressions/transits. In this way, Marjorie can have something to refer to as a guideline as matters develop.

★ ★ ★ ★ ★

Catherine (see also page 78) Moon in Leo in the twelfth, Sun square Saturn in the tenth, had previously been discussing how she had led a very 'rigid' life and had uncovered a pattern of the women in her family dominating and being rigid because they felt that to be so was to be strong. Catherine's Moon in Leo (potentially creative, fun-loving, talented), seems to have been stifled during her upbringing, but following on from the earlier conversation, she has been telling the counsellor of how these qualities seem to be personified in her young son Paul. This twelfth house Moon at the time of consultation was being transited (square) by Uranus and Cathy felt herself being 'more Leo':

Catherine: The difference with me is . . . well you see . . . she was very frustrated, my mother. She had to have everything predictable. Nothing was spontaneous—if there was any kind of disturbance or mess she just couldn't cope with it [♄ 10th—*Cathy had been brought up only by her mother*] And if you had any better ideas than she had, then immediately she'd accuse you of being highfalutin or say you were getting on a hobby horse.

Cllr: Was that directed at you?

Catherine: Oh yes, yes it was always directed at me.

Cllr: So all of this Leo we've talked about had to be subdued?

Catherine: Yes. Talk about being locked away in the twelfth house!

Cllr: Perhaps your mother felt she couldn't allow you to be creative and full of bright ideas because it threatened her in some way? [*focusing on the twelfth house placement*]

Catherine: Oh yes, I think she must have been very unsure about things, bringing us up alone and everything, and covered it by being rigid and well, sort of 'king pin' (☽ ♌).

Cllr: [*Explains at this point the transit of Uranus and how it can emphasize an* awakening *of whatever it touches upon in the chart, in this case the Moon*] Recently you've felt this Leo part of you coming more alive? Perhaps through seeing it in Paul, you're getting more in touch with it as a quality in yourself.

Catherine: Oh *Yes*! [*heavy emphasis*] Oh, its coming out alright. I had a weekend away recently and I had a *marvellous* time [*laughs*] *I really did*! I mean, if Uranus is helping me unbury this Leo of mine, well I tell you I was in my element that weekend . . . I really felt like a Sun Child [*face lights up*] I had a *gorgeous* time!

Cllr: Great! Terrific! Sounds like a great weekend! [*both laugh*]

Catherine: Yes, and what's more, I was in an environment where I was being *praised* for it [*the recognition and acceptance Leo needs*].

★ ★ ★ ★ ★

Thelma has Venus conjunct Neptune ($♀ ☌ ♆$) in Libra ($♎$) which is now transited by Pluto ($♇$) for the second time. Planets may transit two or three times over one particular point, due to their intermittent retrograde motion. It is often found in astrology that when the first transit occurs, the main theme to be incorporated into the person's life emerges quite subtly; then on the second transit it is experienced more forcibly, perhaps as a crisis; later, at a third transit, there is often the resolution of whatever the transit is focusing upon.

In an initial discussion of her chart, Thelma had agreed that she has used this $♀ ☌ ♆ ♎$ in ways which are 'yielding'—frequently she allows herself to be deflected from her course, to 'give up' or 'give in'. By her overwhelming generosity and almost gushing kindness she has frequently been malleable or pliable, easily manipulated and ever-relenting. This has led to situations of much confusion and muddle in Thelma's life and she has already told the counsellor of several instances in which this has been apparent. What interested the counsellor was that on each occasion Thelma's $♀ ♆$ had been activated either by transit or progression.

Now, at this second $♇$ transit, she comes saying that several girls with whom she shares a large flat have been having arguments with her and are leaving. She is terribly worried that she has upset them all by not being very sociable recently, but she has wanted to study in the evenings (a business studies course which she is hoping will help in her career). Now she feels she ought to give it up because it is upsetting everyone else. The counsellor suggests that, with this $♇$ transit, perhaps she *needs* to have people leave so that she can be free to study, but Thelma's overwhelming emotions are more intent on pouring out the story for the moment:

Thelma: Honestly, Nancy came in last night about nine o'clock. I'd only got home myself at eight and had a quick bite to eat and I was just settling down to study when in she comes and goes on and on about this guy she'd been for a drink with, and then she'd been late-night shopping and got some new clothes so she was showing me all these. I mean, they were very nice, but I was getting jumpy because I wanted to get on with studying.

PROGRESSIONS, TRANSITS, AND MAJOR CYCLES 113

Cllr: Could you have explained that to Nancy?

Thelma: Well no! I mean you can't just turn round and say 'Sorry, not interested' can you? I mean she'd bought all these things and was so pleased with them. You can't just turn round and say 'I've got to get on with other things, I haven't got time' can you! [*so ♀ ♇ yielded instead*].

Cllr: I wouldn't have thought that was a good way of going about it, no.

Thelma: And then Brenda . . . she was the one who left last week. Well, she called to pick some things up and [*there follows a long discourse on Brenda*] So anyway, all that took up another half-hour, and then the doorbell went and . . . [*interrupted*]

Cllr: Thelma, it really does sound like it's time for something to go here.

Thelma: Sorry?

Cllr: Yes, it's the Pluto transit I mentioned earlier—I wonder if we could talk about it for a while because I think it has a bearing on what you're saying. [*Thelma nods, so the counsellor again explains the nature of Pluto with its themes of ending something so that something new can begin, particularly as Thelma is keen to do the business studies course which could open up a new direction for her in her career; in addition the ever-solicitous pattern that has been established with the ♀ ☌ ♇ is now being brought into awareness by becoming overwhelming. She does not want to get immersed in what others around are doing yet she is allowing herself to be. Unfortunately, this leaves very little impression on Thelma who seems so bound up in the ♀ ♇ that she tries to plough on with her long discourse on the many interruptions she has.*]

Thelma: As I was saying, I went to the door and it was someone canvassing for a . . . [*interrupted*]

Cllr: Thelma, no. I don't feel this is getting you anywhere nearer to dealing with the main issue of what we've just been talking about.

Thelma: [*Looking a little* ♀ ♆ —*martyred*] Well, I was only going to say that this guy at the door, well he wanted...

Cllr: Yes, I've got the message that there are a lot of interruptions you're allowing in. By telling me the whole story of them you're just increasing the feeling of being overwhelmed, do you see? I also feel you're getting me to collude with it by pulling me in to feel overwhelmed too.

Thelma is looking quite grumpy now, but the counsellor feels she must maintain her confrontation of the ♀ ♆ at the time of this second ♇ transit and be supportive of Thelma's needs at the same time. In this way, Thelma has a greater chance of dealing with it, rather than getting more caught up in its whirlpool, and she may be able to resolve the problems it holds for her when the third transit of ♇ approaches. Otherwise ♇ may need to seek another route, perhaps one of more painful upheaval, to break through Thelma's ♀ ♆:

Thelma: Well, what can you do? I mean I didn't *ask* this guy to come round canvassing.

Cllr: No [*pause*]. But if the door has to be answered at all, could Nancy have gone?—she lives there too.

Thelma: Yes, but she was trying on these new clothes...I *told* you.

Clearly the 'way in' was difficult in this session. When Thelma returned the following week she had not done any studying at all as she had had arguments with Nancy (who had left) and now found that she herself was going to have to leave the flat because she could no longer afford the rent. She added 'I'm beginning to see what you mean about Pluto!' After a month or two of battling financially to pay her debts and back-rent, Thelma was finally able to move into a smaller flat on her own and resolved to take the telephone off the hook during study times. She and the counsellor continued during this period to work together and Thelma looked steadily into the whole question of putting her own needs and those of other people into perspective. By the time ♀ tr. ♀ ♆ for the third time she renewed her wish to embark on the business course and began her studies afresh.

During the period June to December 1980, *Kate* was dealing with three major transits, most of which had a bearing on her relationships with men and all of which were to form key themes for personal work for an extended time thereafter. Saturn (♄) transited the Moon/Neptune conjunction; Uranus (♅) transited in square aspect to both Sun and Aquarius (♒) MC; ♀ transited in square aspect to Mars (♂).

By way of synopsis, Kate has been married and divorced and has had several main relationships since, but in all cases she has ended up being rejected, let-down, disillusioned, as she was in her marriage. Each man she has related to she feels has been in some way weak or negative and Kate has a poignant need for warmth, caring and supportive strength (☉ and ♀ on IC, ♄ ♉, ☽ ♆ 4th) which never seems to be met, in her emotional relationships at any rate.

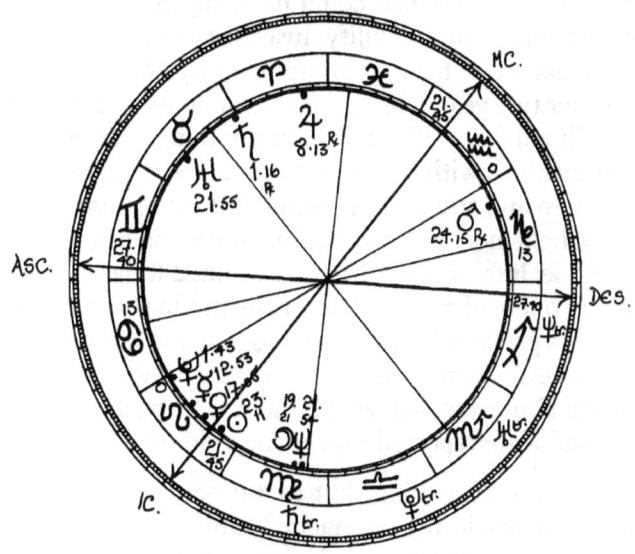

Figure 8. Kate's Chart.

After several lengthy discussions concerning the soft and elusive quality of the ☽ ♆ conjunction in the fourth house with its inner sensitivity, vulnerability and idealism, Kate was able to discern patterns within her of running after her men by seeing to their needs all the time and generally presenting to them her soft, receptive, gentle and tender qualities. However the ♂/♄/♆ T-square also contained feelings of relentless anger and fury which Kate had developed outwardly in ways which would, first subtly and then overtly, put pressure on her men to stay. She demanded and cajoled them into 'knowing where she was' with them (♂ 8th—strong drive to possess in relationships) and when they extricated themselves from this pressure and left, Kate ended up feeling furious with all men. Clearly a very raw spot was being opened to exposure and it was, at this time (with ♄ tr. ☽ ♆), brought to a point of excruciating pain for Kate when yet another man, of whom she had grown very fond, rejected her in favour of someone else. This, together with ♆ tr. □ natal ☽ ☌ ♆, brought Kate to the point of looking into this theme of rejection and loss, which, through studying astrology, she most identified through ☽ ♆ in the fourth.

When discussing this conjunction in terms of Kate's early life, there seemed nothing which could have any bearing on this conjunction's theme of vulnerability, insecurity or loss, and abandonment. Kate had been happily brought up by both parents, along with a brother two years older, through an uneventful, serene and secure childhood (☉ ♀ IC). There was nothing of major difficulty in her relationships with her parents; indeed she got on extremely well with them and still does. It seemed to the counsellor that the conjunction held more of 'the ideal' or 'the wonderful' rather than the negative feeling of rejection Kate seemed to be experiencing. However, a couple of months later, Kate got in touch again to say that a few days previously she had wandered into the kitchen of her mother's house when visiting them one day. They began a conversation about the war years (the war started just after Kate was born) and Kate reported that as they did so:

> It was the strangest thing, but as we began talking I felt this terrible knot inside my stomach. Mum was perfectly calm, I mean she just went on chopping carrots or whatever she was doing as we talked, but I could feel this lump coming up inside

me, up and up, and all of a sudden I just broke down and cried and cried. Mum was good—she just let me cry, and then when I'd finished she said 'I often wondered whether it had any effect on you'.

It emerged that at the outbreak of war, Kate's father had sent her mother to Wales with the two children to be out of London and away from the bombing. Kate's mother was *desperately* lonely without her husband; she was living in a house with someone who was most uncongenial and they did not have enough to eat, nor enough milk for baby Kate. Kate's mother had spent each and every day just sitting and weeping in great despair and loneliness. Of course this was something that very many mothers in those years must have gone through, but this does not negate the fact that for Kate's mother personally the despair was all-enveloping, all-pervading. On hearing of this period, Kate began to feel deeply identified with this painful anguish and was later to say: 'Breaking down and crying like that made me feel very much that Moon/Neptune. I felt I'd picked it all up as that baby, and I've stored it all this time'. One may look at this from the point of view of one situation in childhood causing later experiences, but if we also look upon our nature as putting us into the situations we need, we may also infer that Kate's early experiences were of necessity and purpose as part of her individual path to learning about growth through relationships.

Since the realization of this pattern, with ♄ tr. ☽ ☌ ♆, Kate has been gradually able to focus her life a little more on making concrete changes (with ♅ tr. ☉ and MC), rather than the intense preoccupation of having and keeping a relationship (♀ now transiting the relentless power of the T-square). In the summer of 1981 she started a new business partnership which, by the beginning of 1982, was thriving. This has called forward more of the positive potential of her driving T-square and creative (♌) ability. Kate would still like to find someone with whom she could be in a lasting relationship, but with the charged insistence of it now abating, it is rather more likely that if and when she meets someone else, the relationship can have a greater chance to flourish.

★ ★ ★ ★ ★

Sometimes there is a particular point in a person's life which has the nature of a 'herald'. It calls the person away from life as he knows it in a superficial way, signalling instead an exploration of the deeper purposes of his life. Perhaps several of these points are encountered (sometimes during childhood) before the call to find meaning can be heeded and, since it is fraught with the anxiety of abandoning that which we have been used to, we may ignore it. If we choose to follow it, we face the possibility of much loneliness and lack of understanding from those around us who may never have encountered such a juncture. To some, these particular herald points come through failure, disillusionment, tragedy, suffering—to others they come through being moved by a great work of art, inspired by music or the spoken or written word, galvanized by an heroic act. In whatever way a person is awakened, there is no doubt or tendency to analyse: the illumination is like a flash, which stirs him so deeply that he is held as if spellbound by its authenticity. Crises are more than frequently the avenue through which such movement to deeper meaning comes and the astrological pattern directs us to the nature of that which now works through the person, leading him to a dynamic turning point.

Anna experienced such a moment when she was nineteen. Her childhood and life up until then had been mostly very unhappy. Set against a backdrop of violence between warring parents, she felt intensely lonely and frightened, but somehow 'hung on' (three planets in ♑, ☽☿♀ □ MC, ☿/♇/MC T-square). One of the things that made it easier was an inner certainty she held that it *was* possible to live a life of love and caring amongst people (☽ ☌ ♀, chart ruler ♃ in ♋ 7th ☍ ☉ and ☽). She yearned to find this (☽ ♀ △ ♆) and remained adamant within herself that the background she was experiencing was *not* the true way of living.

Anna had spent the first four years of her life in another country, in a geographical background of much freedom (Asc. ♐ ☌ ♂, Grand Trine Air) and amongst an extended family of grandparents, aunts, uncles, cousins, etc. It is likely that her deeply held values concerning family life and better ways of relating (☉ and ☽ ♑ ☍ ♃ ♋, ♉ IC) were nurtured there, albeit for a short time, and only to be severely tested by enforced removal when the progressed MC came to an exact □ ☿ (☍ ♇), thus mobilizing the whole T-square. Although she does not remember it (and perhaps *because*

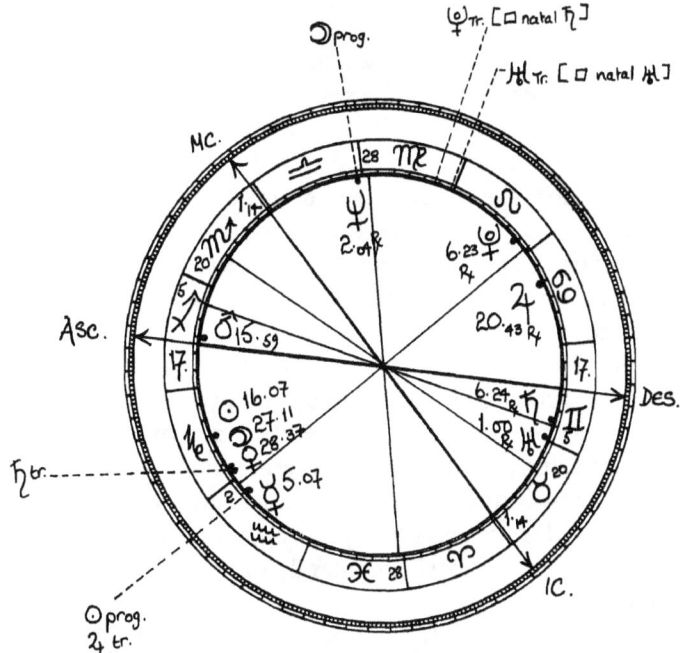

Figure 9. Anna's Chart.

she does not remember it) it seems likely that this disruption had the nature of a personal and cultural shock to Anna.

She was a potentially artistic and intuitive child, at home in the world of make-believe, dance, music, animals, trees and flowers (the Fire and Earth signs which often have a distinctly aesthetic quality to them, ☽ ☿ ♀ △ ♆, ♄ (Ruler of ☉ and ☽ in 6th). She was intelligent, had an inquisitive mind and much enjoyed the freedom of discovery in all things (☿ ♒ △ ♄ ♅ ♆, ☍ ♇, □ ♍ MC, ♄ ♅ ♊). However, few of these things seemed to be valued by her family; rather they were ridiculed, so she dropped them from view, using the elevated ♆ (aspecting major planets) 'more or less to sleepwalk my way through this childhood until the whole ghastly business could be over', crept into a twelfth house ♂, where she nourished considerable anger and resentment (also T-square), and fired on only one cylinder—but quietly.

At seventeen, Anna left home (under a ☽ progressed to □ ♄). Like most seventeen-year olds, she had nothing conscious at the time in terms of what she was doing; all she knew was that the bitterness of family wrangling and brutality was a joy to escape. But she felt very lost, still longing for warmth in a world which seemed only cold and frightening. Yet she was fiercely determined to stay on two feet and be capable (♂ rising, strong ♑ T-square).

At nineteen, the progressions and transits (entered around the rim of Anna's chart) clearly impinge upon the two focal patterns of Grand Trine and T-square; indeed there is scarcely an area of the chart that is unaffected. The T-square involves four planets and the MC; the Grand Trine involves six planets; ☿ is common to both aspect patterns:

The ☉ prog. was ☌ ☿, joining a ♃ transit: The T-square had previously been activated at age four by the prog. MC □ ☿, and this had manifested as Anna's enforced removal from one environment to a less hospitable one. Now at nineteen, the prog. ☉ was again focusing Anna's path into some kind of reconnection with that powerful upheaval (☍ ♇), perhaps in a way that could deepen her awareness (☿) and open her up (♃ tr.) to her next stage of development.

The prog. ☽ was ☌ ♆: This required Anna also to absorb the essence of the whole Grand Trine. Along with ☿ ☍ ♇ 's need to X-ray and get to the nub of things, Anna had constantly tried to search for something that would give her faith, hope, a purpose for which to go on; mostly in her childhood she found this through her dreams of a better world, through Christian prayer ('Not that I understood it,' she said, 'it just felt right to me as a child... talking to God'.) and by communing with nature and especially animals. As well as ♆ in the ninth house and ♃ ☍ ☉ ☌ ☽ (both containing themes of needing to find a sense of meaning), the three earth planets and their ruler (♄) in the sixth house seem important here. Being an earth house, the sixth can often contain themes of growth via contact through the senses (as can ♍, the sixth sign). Perhaps it is for this reason that older astrological textbooks list small animals as coming under the sixth house, for the importance of touch and warmth between human beings and their pets is well known at times of physical or psychological ill-being. Like, perhaps, many children who feel under stress with no-one to understand, Anna would often go to a favourite tree, or stone, or animal to bear innermost feelings. But now, at nineteen, she was alone in the world and isolated from those earlier 'playmates', and very much feeling it.

PROGRESSIONS, TRANSITS, AND MAJOR CYCLES 121

♄ *transited the* ☽ ☌ ♀ : This conjunction had initially received much warmth and a sense of belonging, but later felt abandoned. Now it was focused upon again via the ♄ theme of construction. Anna knew nothing about facing vulnerability and fear and, at this age, may not have been able to do so anyway. Feeling alone, isolated and a victim of her early environment, Anna tried to build for herself (♄) a sense of belonging (☽) by attempting a reconciliation with the only home and family she could reach. Having left home two years previously she now made a weekend visit.

♇ *transited* □ *to* ♄ *in the 6th:* The brute power of ♇ in conflict with the individual's defences—a rather relentless, pressurizing energy which requires a person to clench teeth and dig deep, usually through experiencing a heavy test of strength, physical, psychological, spiritual. For Anna, with three planets in ♑ and their ruler (♄) now being transited in an Earth house, this period was one where she was to learn the first of many lessons about letting go of defences and controls. This kind of test of strength, shattering though it is, heralds a necessary prelude to the transformative aspect of ♇ 's nature which can lead the individual to the birth of a new awareness, a new phase in life.

♅ *transited in* □ *to its natal place:* This is a very important cycle reaching exactness during the ages of 19-22 years and it is accompanied by a □ of ♄ to its natal place at roughly age 21. At this juncture of life, the individual has gone through adolescence with all of its battles for 'identity' and initial struggles away from the sanctuary of home, family, parents. And yet, with the approach of the ♄ □, and having fought for one's own path, there are now social values to which the individual needs to conform and place himself in some other kind of 'niche'.

So the achievement of independence and also the need still to 'root' oneself set the tone of this period and can be felt as a conflict. Independence may be achieved physically, but we still want a haven to run back to at this age. Rebellion against adult/parental values may now be diluted with some acceptance of them as the individual becomes adult himself. Many young people are leaving University during this period to start their first careers, or they may already be working; some may also now start to think about marriage and settling into the creation of homes/havens of their own.

For Anna, the conflict between independence and stability is particularly highlighted by the ♄ ☌ ♅ in the sixth house (now under transit). This conjunction was present in the charts of everyone born between 1941/43 and assumes different levels of personal importance according to the rest of the chart. In Anna's chart, ♄ and ♅ between them are the rulers of four of the personal planets—☉, ☽, ☿ and ♀. At this time, Anna had a job and, although she had a boyfriend, she entertained no thoughts of marriage. She had achieved some measure of independence in leaving home and making new friendships among people she worked with, many of whom held similar interests to her (and which she had hitherto had little freedom to express) and she was generally liked and valued. But she felt deeply the lack of stable roots from a family (♉ on the IC, ♀ in ♑ now also transited by ♄).

So, overall, for Anna this period was one of powerful upheaval which could lead to deeper awareness (☉ p☌ ☿ and ♃ tr.), an inner need to reconnect with faith, a sense of purpose (☽ p☌♆), facing emotional vulnerability and fears (♄ tr. ☽ ♀ ♑), the shattering of defences and emergence into the adult world on the terms she had so far been able to build up (♇ tr. □ ♄ 6th, ♅ □ ♅ cycle).

As mentioned earlier, Anna went for a weekend visit to her family. Not only did she find the old pattern of fierce violence and hostility amongst them intact, but it now became directed solely at her. It left Anna physically, and psychically, bloody and bruised by the end of the first day. Late at night she ran all the way home to the small bedsitter she lived in and, once again in her life, she was in shock and quite quite terrified. It was a very cold December night; Anna had no food in as she had expected to be away for the weekend and she was penniless, as she had given what she had, after paying rent, to her family for her upkeep. To Anna it was 'the pit', a dark torturous hole she had sometimes experienced in dreams during childhood. Cold, hungry, bloody and bowed she decided to take her own life.

She threw herself down on her bed to cry some last anguished sobs; she does not know how long she cried but remembers being convulsed in uncontrollable grief and fear, still bleeding from her wounds and hurting badly from bruises. There was no one else present in the building at all, nobody to whom she could turn. Thus, again, there is the theme of this kind of herald requiring the person to be alone to receive it. Suddenly, Anna felt the atmosphere change in a way she cannot explain, but the instinctive reaction of her ☽ ♑ was to 'play dead'—one of those controlled defence manoeuvres she had cultivated in order to survive during childhood. This lasted only a second or two and then she let the blanket with which she was covering her face fall away; inexplicably she felt very very warm, somehow very calm and terribly safe. She does not remember anything after that, except falling into a very deep sleep and waking well into the next day charged with the unmistakable knowledge that her life had meaning and purpose. She did not bother with the 'hows' or 'whys', indeed they did not occur to her; she simply knew that something greater than herself, deeper than the Anna she knew, had taken over from within and shown her that the only way for her life was onwards; that if she wanted to find the way of life she believed was possible, then it was up to her to start creating and living it. In retrospect, Anna was to say that she felt this was a first point in the transmutation of the energy she herself had poured into keeping her own hostility and vengefulness intact. By becoming the recipient of it via the actions of her family it almost shattered her, but yet transformed her into being able to say 'yes' to life.

OTHER CYCLES IN LIFE:
Saturn: Uranus: Neptune: Pluto

One person's cold-and-alone-December-night turning point is but one way of the individual progressing on to a different path in life. There are very many others, and the astrological chart provides an insight into the cycles and patterns of development that lie behind them. A retrospective astrological look at key junctures in life often helps a person make sense of what occurred in the past, and why. It can also help him make sense of the present, for it is often the case that today's situation has connections with yesterday's experience.

The Saturn and Uranus cycles at around age twenty-one provide a turning point at which the individual confirms for himself that he is emerging as a person of consequence in the world. He is doing adult things like getting a job, driving cars, drinking alcohol, marrying, voting, fighting for his country—all with society's consent. He is now deemed a person of responsibility; at least, he goes through the motions. He will probably also set targets for himself which he aims to achieve in the next ten years.

However, it is not until he reaches the age of approximately twenty-nine, when *Saturn returns* by transit to its natal position, that the individual truly stands up to be counted in terms of his personal responsibility for his life and direction from now on. By this time, the horizons he envisaged for himself earlier at twenty-one may have been reached, or they may appear a little too distant for him to attain realistically, or be shrouded in mist altogether because they have progressively become less important or ineffective in terms of the way he is developing. The urge at this point in life is to establish and strike out upon a new road altogether in some way. The underlying feeling is that, in comparison to this new road, past ones have been lacking in personal, individual meaning for him; so he makes an adjustment to restructure his life in a different way.

One of the key themes during this age twenty-nine phase is a sense of release. Frequently this is because the person can now begin to realize that his life is in his hands and he can truly construct it for himself from now on. He begins to get a glimpse of himself as the weaver of the tapestry and can now start to unravel the tangled webs amongst it all. He may be led to this realization through a negative crisis (career failure, illness, divorce, for instance) or he may pass through a very successful period, or one of great emotional happiness. There may be no 'outer' changes apparent at all, but only inner emotional and psychological adjustments which precipitate the 29-year-old into saying things like 'Oh I don't know, things are changing. I just feel I want to make a fresh start somehow'. Whatever the turning point consists of, the individual is now required to adjust his life to strive for full maturity, increased productiveness, personal responsibility and adherence to his own values as opposed to social/parental ones by which he defined himself in the past. A platform of self-determination is now the order of the day.

The transition from life's morning to life's afternoon means a reassessment of one's earlier values.

(Alexander Ruperti)

At later cyclic turning points in our lives, we are faced with anxieties which might be called 'existential'. We have them because we are alive, because we are *being*. Of these, there is the ever-present anxiety that, because we are alive, there is always the inevitability of our death facing us. In our younger years this is a purely cognitive notion, but at some point it hits us rather more profoundly. All of a sudden, advertisements suggesting we consider pension schemes and retirement policies seem very appealing and are taken note of, and policemen all start to look terribly young. The beginning of recognizing such inevitability as a personal reality is often a feature of the mid-life period (roughly 35-44 years) which, astrologically, marks the time when *Uranus* in its 84-year cycle around the zodiac reaches the point opposite its natal place. The nine-year time scale has been noted by Elliot Jaques writing on the mid-life crisis in *Work Creativity and Social Justice*,* but although the ripples of this cycle's implications can extend over this whole period, a crescendo is usually experienced around 39-42 years.

As we have seen with Uranus, its nature is one of change leading us on to a transition (Neptune) and transformation (Pluto). We break through established patterns into new spheres of expression, spheres which have hitherto lain fallow. We can either 'snivel and back way' (to requote Lawrence) or we can make our way through the 'hole in the wall and find a new world outside'. Synonymous with Uranus' nature there are many variations upon how this can manifest in an individual's life. The most common underlying theme is a paradoxical one of both gain and loss. We have been striving all through our 20s and 30s and now, around 40, we reach a crest. Perhaps we have achieved a great deal in our lives up until this time, and/or we may now awaken to something within us that could launch us into a new and creative period. We are particularly prone to taking completely new roads altogether, some of which may be sudden and dramatic. There is a reversal of activities, temperament, interests, outlooks, etc., by which we endeavour to liberate ourselves from life as we knew it before and experience a new vista. At the same time, however, something else (such as the death of a parent or the sudden realization that our children are grown up) gives us a gentle (or not-so-gentle!) reminder that time is indeed going by.

For most of us change is disruptive and we may attempt to dam up the hole in the wall and try to get things back to how they were.

*Heinemann, 1970.

Time passing by is something we usually fear because the advance towards the closing periods of our lives leads us to think of things which are devalued in our society—the approach of old age and eventual death are invariably linked to the concept of deterioration rather than seen as a valuable means of development. Thus, at this mid-life stage, men and women start to scrabble around for what they feel are last chances. Physically, questions of potency, virility, sagging chins and disappearing waistlines loom large. Emotionally, too, we feel time is running out and we may search for relationships that we feel will restore to us the sense of being loved, appreciated, beautiful, desirable.

Most importantly, the way we have come through past cycles in our lives will also have a bearing on how we deal with this one; mature adulthood may re-present itself as a main task. Needs which have not been worked through at much earlier stages (such as adolescence) now endeavour to surface within the human psyche again. New relationships now formed on the basis of these needs may well flounder since an adolescent approach is inappropriate to the age the person has now reached. Similarly, if he is still conforming to social/parental values, having failed to disengage earlier to create an individual path for himself, these too may confront the individual in some way, requiring him to change them. He may, for instance, find that his children persist in overtly rebellious, anti-social behaviour in contrast to his propriety and slavish adherence to social acceptability.

Each of these cycles of Saturn, Uranus, Neptune and Pluto could each fill a book on their own, but this Uranus cycle at around age forty is especially important since it is closely followed by cycles of the remaining outer planets. *Saturn* opposes its natal position for the second time in one's life around age forty-four, requiring us to test the truth of the situations we live and the way we live them; *Neptune* forms a square to its natal position around the same time and then, similarly, *Pluto* is in square to natal Pluto.

During the Neptune cycle, great feelings can be stirred within Neptunian themes of yearning for something of greater ultimate value. The person may begin to feel he has wasted his life, or that somehow it all lacks meaning. He endeavours to glimpse something beyond his earthbound experiences, particularly in the light of whatever bits and pieces are left over from his breakthrough in the Uranian mid-life period. Having not quite reached my fortieth birthday, I cannot speak from personal life-experience of the Neptune and Pluto cycles, but among the people I have worked with as clients, I am learning that themes of both 'loss' and 'bliss' can occur when Neptune squares its natal place. Most often, for those who are married and have brought up a family, there is either a poignant sense of 'What do we do now the children are gone?', or 'Isn't it wonderful the children have flown the nest and we can be a couple again!'. In the first instance, husband and wife may suddenly look at one another again after twenty or so years of having always had the children in the foreground, and find to their dismay that they do not know how to relate to one another as people any more. In the second instance, they are likely to be booking airline tickets to take them on a second honeymoon. People who have lived marriage and parenthood as 'roles' now may find that Neptune undermines the structure of that role until it is corroded; as Pluto merges into a square aspect to its natal place, they may find the role breaks down altogether and the individual begins to question himself concerning issues of power, maintenance and destruction in his life.

With Pluto square to Pluto, a main theme which arises is how the person has used *his own* power in life, creatively or otherwise, and also what his self-destructive or self-defeating patterns have consisted of. Unresolved issues from a long way back may emerge to be dealt with and/or Pluto's theme of intensity and power may be met in some form amongst people he relates to. Sometimes people around the age of fifty or so find a powerful level of sexuality emerging within them which they might find unsettling—or a pleasant surprise!—or, in an existing relationship, they may find that power changes hands in some way.

Although all of these cycles can only be touched upon here, the emerging rhythms of life as we move from one phase to another are of crucial importance in understanding the content and process of our lives. The astrological counsellor who is aware of these cycles can be of help to the person passing through them, guiding him to tread the path to fulfillment and completion, which leads healthily to the next phase of life. For further reading on the cycles of our lives, the reader is particularly referred to *Cycles of Becoming: The Planetary Pattern of Growth* by Alexander Ruperti (see Appendix I).

Most often the cycles of our lives from mid-life onwards are those that require us to look inside ourselves rather than shore up exterior appearances; it is helpful if a person comes to the astrological counsellor a little while prior to such cycles so that the counsellor can allow for some discussion of its advent and thus help the client become aware of it; this then relieves the pressure of it building up unnoticed. The preparation of a client for an impending cycle does not, however, have to take the nature of a 'warning'— after all, it was *fresh* air that was streaming through Lawrence's 'hole in the wall'.

PART 3: THE ASTROLOGER'S FRAMEWORK: THE CLIENT'S NEEDS

9.
FIRST STEPS TO CONSULTATION

As most people know, there are three pieces of information an astrologer needs in order to calculate a birth chart: the full date, the exact time and the location of birth. If the birth time is uncertain or unknown, it is better for the client to make every endeavour to find this out beforehand. Mothers/fathers/aunts/uncles/older brothers and sisters often prove remarkable in their memory of an event that occurred years past, and so these are the obvious people to check with first. Birth times are not recorded on certificates for babies born in England, Wales and Northern Ireland, unless they are born a twin, but they are in Scotland and in many countries abroad. Hospitals and Nursing Homes often keep records long after a birth has occurred, so they too are worth a letter of enquiry.

If, after such researches, it is impossible to ascertain the time of birth, the astrologer may be willing to work with a chart for the day of birth only and can explain to the client what this will mean, i.e. what will be missing from the chart because of the absence of a precise time. Sometimes if the time is known but vaguely, the astrologer may be able to deduce the actual moment of birth by a process known as 'rectification', but this is not infallible and can be a time-consuming task, so other avenues for discovering a birth time should be followed first.

The chart once calculated and drawn up, it is important for the astrological counsellor to hear what it is within the client's life that has precipitated him into asking for a consultation. There is often a specific problem or question the client is raising about himself, or a particular area of his life upon which he would like to focus when working with the counsellor, e.g. his relationships or his career. It is a question I always ask my own clients when they contact me, for the danger of not doing so can mean that the astrologer will simply launch into an interpretation of the chart from her own viewpoint only, perhaps only skimming over or bypassing altogether that which the client has really come for.

Often, of course, a client may find it extremely difficult to pinpoint reasons, for they may not as yet be accessible to his conscious awareness and thus he is unable to formulate them in precise language. Human beings can frequently be a whole jumble of feelings and cannot state with clarity what is only experienced as a welter of anxieties, perplexities, sadnesses and agitations. In this situation, it is not uncommon for the client to say 'Well, I don't know, I just feel a bit restless' or 'Well, it's difficult to say, but I just have the feeling I need to make some changes in my life' or 'I don't really have any aims, I'm just drifting'. Of course, clients may simply say 'No, there's no special reason, it's just for general interest'. All these responses are entirely understandable and accepted by the astrological counsellor; indeed she would regard it as part of her function to help the client focus with greater clarity upon more specific avenues to which his searching may be taking him.

Beyond knowing the client's full birth data and the general, or specific, aim he has for consulting the astrological counsellor, the latter needs to know a little about him—not a full life story, but some brief background history. Some people assume they must be as mysterious as possible when consulting an astrologer and it is for the latter magically to divulge facts and events in the client's life that no one else could possibly have known. This is irrelevant to astrological counselling and is as ridiculous as visiting a doctor saying 'First, guess what's wrong with me, then see if you can cure me'.

To understand the need for some background information, it is useful to draw an analogy. Perhaps if you can imagine that a man is driving on a long journey from one city to another and at some point he loses his way. He telephones a motoring organization saying 'I'm in my car travelling from Manchester to Plymouth and I'm lost'. The first thing the person on the other end of the line is going to ask is 'Well, where are you now?' And that is what the astrological counsellor needs to know—where is the client in his life at the moment? He may be thirty years old and want to be pointed in a particular direction in his life, just as our motorist needed pointing in the direction of Plymouth; but the counsellor is placed in an unnecessarily difficult situation if she is given no knowledge of what the client's 'journey' has consisted of so far and his present 'location'. These are not factors which can be instantly read from the astrological map, for that map shows us the 'route' but does not tell us how much or how little of it has been so far travelled.

Another important reason for this background information is that, without it, the astrological counsellor may be in danger of assuming that her client's life is like her own, runs on the same lines, and that the client sees and deals with life and reality on an identical level to her. Much of this ground will be covered when the counsellor and client meet and the work together begins, but it should be remembered that the astrological counsellor is dealing with a planetary map of basic energies which find their setting in many different experiences and situations. What appears in the sky as a simple outline of potential takes on many different facets and manifestations when lived out by the individual. It is by talking with the individual that their *actual* setting in his life becomes clear.

10.
INTERPRETATION AND COUNSELLING

It can often be confusing both for astrologer and client to know where interpretation ends and counselling begins, and indeed what the difference is between the two. Throughout this book I have interchanged the words 'astrologer', 'astrological counsellor' and 'counsellor', but it is important for each astrologer to decide clearly what is meant when referring to themselves as astrological counsellors. If this means they interpret charts and deliver advice to the client based on that information, then this is chart analysis/interpretation rather than counselling.

As we have seen earlier, there has been a tremendous pressure on astrologers (as well as a willingness on their part) to provide constant 'proofs' of astrology by displaying their ability to describe accurately the characteristics and life pattern of the person who is their client; it is intriguing for the client and a feather in the cap of the astrologer. But if we are truly to use astrology for self-understanding we need to take a closer look at what, and who, this overt interpretation is actually for. An astrology which purports to be an aid to psychological development and growth and then proceeds to dump rigid interpretations upon a mute client is no aid at all. A birth chart 'reading' in these circumstances becomes all too often something a person has done and forgets about the following week. Moreover, can it really be sensible to try to guess definite outcomes of planetary configurations, or is it not infinitely more wholesome to put the client in touch with their essential principles so that he can become aware of their *actual* relevance in his life and share this with someone who is prepared to listen?

In astrological counselling, the interpretations made by the counsellor are not of an inflexible nature nor are they delivered wholesale upon her client. Of course she may well have a keen insight into the way a particular configuration is working in her client's life, but she is primarily concerned with her client's experience of it and helping him 'centre' to the process underlying it. One person with Mars conjunct Saturn in the fourth house may have had a harsh, cold and tyrannical father; another may have come from a family of physical fitness experts; the underlying process in each situation is that of discipline.

The counsellor therefore needs to resist making premature interpretations of chart factors before she has built up an understanding of the actual lines upon which the client lives his life; apart from anything else, she may be wrong and therefore be proceeding along no more than the lines of her own erroneous assumptions. More importantly, because it is a two-way shared relationship, interpretations can be effected by the counsellor and client *together*, by the counsellor describing the principles underlying chart factors and inviting the client, with her help, to reflect upon their particular meaning in his life. More than anything else, through the counsellor listening to and conversing with the client, the chart is automatically 'interpreted', for the client is speaking it, living it, being it.

Very often the chart can become superfluous and it becomes a matter of talking with the client without that piece of paper constantly being referred to. The latter can be particularly off-putting to a client who is endeavouring to convey a deep worry, or frustration, or fear and if the chart is avidly scrutinized at every word he utters, every move he makes, it can make him abandon the work with the astrologer altogether.

If the client has not brought a particular problem but is there for a general chart interpretation, a counselling approach to this is still possible, i.e. in ways which allow him to find his own level of experience of chart factors and to emerge at the end of the session with a coverage of his chart with which he can work for a period of time afterwards, or intermittently as he develops through his life. Again, taking a particular chart factor, the astrologer can offer several possibilities for its manifestation in his life; the client can choose the one which 'sits straight' for him in his life as he knows it and has experienced it so far. For example, a Moon conjunct Saturn in the fourth house of a chart can suggest an inner feeling of loneliness in a person's nature; possibly he felt very alone as a child and may still feel isolated at times. Sometimes people with this aspect in their charts have experienced a sense of rejection, or deprivation, lack of love, feeling apart from any deep sense of belonging, so they might have had to create this sense for themselves. There may also have been the experience of hardship or difficulty in life, which may still colour their current situations; perhaps they have had to develop a great amount of endurance, capability, toughness or practicality in life or have trodden a path of 'going it alone', developed a strong inner sense of responsibility, duty, constancy, and so on. Astrological textbooks are full of good advice to the astrologer on what else to look for and other techniques to use in order to make more definite interpretations but few, if any, of them suggest that the client could be asked. But by doing so it may even arise that a particular configuration has an altogether different bearing in the client's life than any the astrologer or her books have thought to suggest. The important factor is that the client is included in the interpretation—it does not take place at a distance from him and he is left with the power to make his own choices.

Some astrologers will state explicitly what their set pattern is for working with clients, or what their goal and intentions are in going over the chart with him. To an extent, this is necessary since the astrologer needs to have a clear 'job-definition', which can be explained to the potential client so that her framework and his expectations can coincide. However, I do not feel that the astrologer can be dogmatic about what is to occur, simply because the experience of the session is not hers alone. Clients too come with their own intentions of what they are going to get out of the consultation (whether those intentions are conscious or not) and often they may not parallel those the astrologer may have set her heart on. She may feel that it is her job to make the client aware of this T-square or that conjunction, but it may well turn out that such a goal is inappropriate to the client for those chart factors may not relate to an issue currently pressing upon him (though that is not to say they will not arise at some other time). What is important is that if the astrologer sets definite goals, she needs to be aware of whether the chart factors she wants to focus on to achieve these goals actually do impinge upon the client's current needs and experience, or indeed have more to do with her own. Another way in which this can frequently be met is for the astrologer one day to be reading a brilliant interpretation in a book of, say, Mars conjunct Pluto in the eighth house—and, hey presto, the very next client to come to her has Mars conjunct Pluto in the eighth house! The need can be enormous to impart to the client all of the brilliance and insight she has discovered in that book—only to find that it falls on ears which are deaf to it, at least for the moment, since it has little or no current relevance for the client. He may also not be at a point in his development where he can bring these factors into consciousness anyway.

Being wedded to textbook interpretations can also detract from what the client is actually saying. Jane, who has a Grand Trine of Sun/Ascendant/Jupiter in her chart, had gone through a long period of depression which worried her greatly and she consulted an astrologer. She was told that because of this Grand Trine (which was faithfully interpreted as happy, jovial, lucky, optimistic, etc.) she had no business to be grumbling and that it was 'just what the doctor ordered'. Jane was to remark to me later 'Actually, what the doctor ordered was 15mg Valium, 20mg Tofranol, 25mg ampitriptilyne, bed rest in hospital and a visit from the psychiatrist there'!

As a general pattern of working with clients, it is also frequently found that very little can be achieved in a single session. Several meetings over a period of weeks (or months) can often be more appropriate for the astrologer and client to work together and discover deeper meanings from the chart. Some astrological counsellors work at deeper levels still, as psychotherapists for instance, where the scope of work can extend over much longer periods of time if necessary. But if she does not practise in this way, the counsellor may (if appropriate) refer the client to such a psychotherapist, having provided sufficient supportive counselling to enable him to clarify the issues he is striving to resolve. It is up to the individual counsellor to define for herself what her experience, abilities and training do, or do not, enable her to provide for her client. Some (basic at the very least) counselling training is necessary for the astrologer, for a qualification in astrology itself does not automatically imply counselling ability.

When clients initially come for a general chart interpretation, my own approach (which is not necessarily that of other astrological counsellors and which may also vary according to the client) is to begin the work by describing the main themes to emerge from the chart. There are usually at least two or three which run a thread through the client's general life experience and with which he can usually instantly identify. By drawing these threads together, the counsellor and client have a basic 'platform' from which to explore the deeper aspects of each theme, how they have been experienced and what they now bring to light. Often it can happen that they come across something in the chart which is of supreme relevance at the current time and the rest of the session is spent discussing this. Alternatively, after initial coverage of the whole chart has been completed, the client may feel that there are a few main issues which have emerged from it which he would like to discuss further, and in such cases further counselling sessions can be arranged.

Some astrologers feel they simply must interpret every single little nook and cranny of the chart—every midpoint, every semi-sextile, every tiny transit and in so doing engulf the client in a whirlpool of information he has no hope of really finding useful—neither can he cope with the sheer fatigue! There is so much we can go on and on finding out from our charts, I do not believe that it is either possible or necessary to deal with everything in one fell swoop and beleaguer ourselves and our clients in the process. The awarenesses a chart can offer us naturally develop in the course of time anyway, and not necessarily in one instant.

11.
FINDING SOLUTIONS TO PROBLEMS

A person presents a problem but does not know what to do about it. Frequently (and again largely due to the way astrology is popularly presented) people approach an astrological counsellor with the assumption that the latter, equipped with Special Inside Knowledge derived from the birth chart, must know what the solution to the problem is. Sadly, many astrologers will happily fall in with this assumption and take on the role of an authority figure, proferring advice on exactly what to do, and when. By so doing, the client's experience of himself as being incapable of solving problems by himself is escalated. He believes that he is somehow weak or negative because of this and, moreover, the astrologer who takes on the role of Problem Solver draws a subtle but clearly defined picture of the client as one whose life must be lived according to the dictates of others, especially her. If an astrologer is one who maintains old astrological images of 'bad' aspects, malevolent stars and a precisely set future awaiting you, the dependency of the client is aggravated by a deep-rooted sense of fear and trepidation.

It is, of course, understandable when people exhibit a great need for someone to tell them how to get out of an awful predicament, what the magical something is that will set a relationship right, which of two courses to pursue, how to stop feeling angry, or depressed, or inferior, and so on. There can surely be few of us who have not reached such a point of exasperation in our lives and in some instances people need fast and practical interventions by another person to help them handle, say, a severe crisis. However, it is also the case that in astrological counselling all the above needs can be unhelpfully catered for by an astrology which promises to 'reveal all' and plot the most important events you are going to meet.

Any 'advice' in astrological counselling is given in terms of guidance as opposed to instruction. As mentioned earlier telling a person what to do leads both to negative dependency and robs him of his own decisive power. Whether a client should or should not change his job, get a divorce, go on a long trip, and so forth, should be left to him to settle; with the counsellor's help he can work this out for himself by clarifying the different choices which might be made, recognizing and accepting any negative feelings in connection with these and coming to new insights which can help him move ahead to a different way of looking at the situation, all of which the birth chart, current progressions, transits and cycles will clarify.

Information may sometimes need to be given to a client, such as telling him how he can find his nearest marriage guidance centre, where to get specialized help with drinking problems/drug addiction/sexual difficulties, etc., or it may be that part of a problem he raises would be better referred to a legal or financial or other kind of consultant. Guidance can also be offered in terms of other forms of personal psychological growth-oriented work which the counsellor may feel could help the client move nearer a satisfactory conclusion for himself, although it would be unfair to make suggestions willy-nilly without personal knowledge or experience on the counsellor's part. Neither can she view the client's problem only through her own day-to-day experience of living, perhaps identifying it as a situation she has gone through at some stage and then giving advice based on those things or on what she thinks is the commonsense method of dealing with it anyway.

The difficulties we experience in life emerge from layers within us, made up of intricate mazes of feelings, events, thoughts, memories, insights, intuitions, assumptions, and so on. Thus, presenting a problem does not necessarily mean that there is a slick sure-fire answer which will sweep it away and that all you have to do is to go to the astrological counsellor who will tell you what it is. Any 'answers' emerge from entering the maze and following its various interconnected paths. Most frequently it is found that the main components of the problem cannot be tackled from the level

FINDING SOLUTIONS TO PROBLEMS

upon which they are experienced and described and, additionally, insights can frequently emerge from the individual following a totally different avenue from the one he started off with.

More than frequently when we have a problem, we immediately want to 'reach up to a shelf', as it were, and take down the 'remedy bottle', without allowing ourselves the time to look into what the problem is composed of and, indeed, what it might *offer* us. In short, a 'simple problem' of shall I? shan't I? how do I? what's the best way to? when will I? and so on, opens up to a road of multitudinous personal assumptions and feelings which, while remaining untrodden, prevents us from moving any nearer to a conclusion which would also help us progress.

Natasha is forty-three years old, divorced, with two sons aged seventeen and fifteen. She comes to the astrological counsellor specifically with the problem of being undecided as to what she should do with her life—whether to continue being mostly at home and find temporary part-time work, or whether to search for and build up a full-time career. She says on the telephone 'I feel I'm going round and round in circles and not getting anywhere—I just don't know what *to do*!'

As well as considering the birth chart, the counsellor also notes the current transits and progressions, in particular those which could have a bearing on what Natasha is experiencing. These are shown on the outer perimeter of the chart (Figure 10) and the three major chart developments are ♅ tr. ☍ ♅ (see page 125) and both ♄ and ♀ transiting the Midheaven.

Both of these two latter transits suggest a need within the individual to establish and consolidate her position in the outer world through the use of her own power and effort in some way. They hold the possibility of a complete transformation or turning point for Natasha, coupled with the opportunity to demonstrate her capacity for personal responsibility and a mature approach to the fulfilment of tasks. Whether she will stand or fall in any of this remains to be seen, but the counsellor can draw on the birth chart to focus on possible qualities which Natasha might mobilize at this phase of her development. There is a potentially capable and responsible Sun in Capricorn, with Mercury square Saturn (construc-

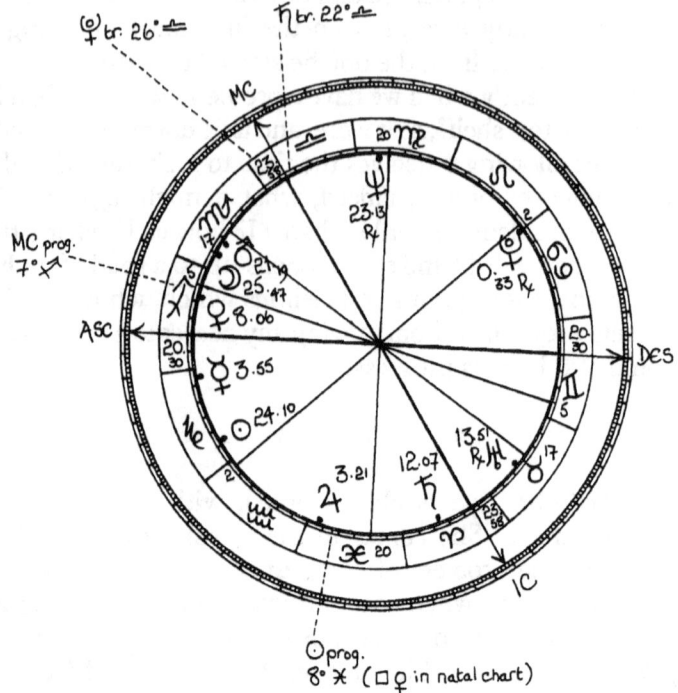

Figure 10. Natasha's Chart.

tive method and practicality), plus Moon conjunct Mars in Scorpio, suggesting a strong personal drive and dynamic committment to whatever she is engaged upon.

Additionally, it is noted that the Libra MC by progression is now approaching a conjunction to the natal Venus (♀), Ruler of Libra (♎). This is coupled with a progression of ♀ itself to the natal Sun. Thus the themes of both ♀ and ♎ are accentuated, further suggesting that Natasha's personal values (♀) in life are emerging for clarification and presentation to the world at large (MC, tenth house), perhaps in terms of her capacity for work and achievement (also MC, tenth house, Sun in Capricorn, the tenth sign) and personal resources (♀ natural ruler of the second house), or in terms of interpersonal relationships (♀ and ♎ natural ruler of seventh house)—or indeed all of these themes.

These outline processes could be brought 'down to the ground' so to speak and overtly interpreted for Natasha. She might be

FINDING SOLUTIONS TO PROBLEMS 145

advised to start in earnest to find a career and use those strong capabilities shown in her chart. Some might build up on that advice and predict that she has some good things coming up emotionally: perhaps now that her children are grown she will have more freedom and find a new relationship. All of those may well be so, but astrological factors refer to types of experience for which there can be many possibilities and it is not for the astrologer to lay upon the client a specific scenario as she sees it, but to describe what is involved so that the client has a wider awareness from which to make choices.

In short, we may look upon this developmental phase in Natasha's life as a potential testing point for her capabilities and emotional values, but it is already clear that it is not a simple matter of getting on with it, for she has already said she is going round in circles and does not know what to do. It also becomes clear when talking with her that her route to clarifying the issues involved and experiencing these themes is indeed circuitous, touching off several other 'byroads', all of which have a bearing upon and colour her approach to the situation she is in:

Cllr: You said on the telephone, Natasha, that you're going round in circles and not getting anywhere.

Natasha: Yes, I can't decide whether to get a full-time job or not. The whole idea of going out into the world and having a main career, you know something that's going to keep me there eight hours or so every day . . . well, I must say it frightens me . . . or whether I should get a part-time job, do bits and pieces here and there and earn enough just to keep going, and still be around, at home, I mean, for the kids and so on. Oh, I don't know, I just don't know what to *do*! [*looking very agitated, twisting a handkerchief round and round in her hands*].

Sometimes at this point it can be very easy to launch straight into 'Well, your charts shows . . .' but it is important for the client, particularly if she is feeling agitated, to know that she is being understood and for the counsellor to take time to convey this. Additionally, it was important in Natasha's case to postpone for the moment any overt interpretation of the chart since, on the face of it, both the birth chart and the current transits suggest the basic ability to cope with and a supreme opportunity for the very thing Natasha says she finds frightening.

Cllr: So a full-time job is frightening because it's a big undertaking, although you'd earn more. But a part-time job, well with that you could be at home too, but you'd earn just enough to keep going.

Natasha: Yes, part-time feels better—but I can't find anything at the moment . . . but, well it would only be *bits* of work and I don't know whether that's very fulfilling. I mean I'd earn something, but—well, it's not really achievement is it?

Cllr: And what *would* be achievement—a full-time job which kept you there eight hours a day? . . .

Natasha: Yes.

Cllr: Yes, I see, which frightens you.

Natasha: Yes, do you know I really admire women of thirty or so who've built up a business, or are their own boss. I think that's terrific, but the thought of *me* doing that . . . well! goodness . . . I mean—I used to work in television and I went down to the studios the other day to see if there was anything going by way of part-time jobs, but getting into that scene again I could see I'd be there till all hours and have very little time for anything else. I wouldn't be free during the day at all . . . Now, if I want to take off somewhere during the day I can.

Cllr: Your chart certainly points up a good number of factors that suggest there's a lot of capability in you for achievement, building up a career [*they go briefly over the Capricorn, Moon/Mars in Scorpio content together*] but at the same time you seem to be saying that it's not only frightening [*Natasha nods*] but that there are other priorities too—priorities you want to be free for during the day?

Natasha: [*Takes several rapid breaths*] Yes—yes, well . . . it's *the* priority actually. I'm in a relationship which is important to me. He's married you see, so I can usually only see him during the day. I don't want *not* to see Peter, and you see I wouldn't be able to if I was working eight hours a day.

Peter is discussed a little longer at this point since, for Natasha, he is '*the* priority'. Natasha tells the counsellor Peter wants to remain married, but he also likes to have her in his life. This is not acceptable to Natasha and causes her a great deal of distress since she wants a relationship of much deeper emotional involvement (☽ ☌ ♂ ♏). Bearing in mind the advent of MC progressed to ♀ and ♀ progressed ☌ ☉ this line is followed, but mostly because it is upsetting to Natasha, which she now clearly demonstrates by crying. She tells the counsellor all about the relationship and, after listening, the counsellor gradually endeavours to help Natasha clarify what the relationship means for her; knowing that she is unable to have a closer involvement with Peter, what holds her there? What are the relationship's main values for her? What might its purpose be? Much time has elapsed by now and eventually Natasha says:

Natasha: One thing about Peter is that he really feels that I *can*, he really feels I'm *able*—he *likes* my capabilities.

Cllr: Sounds like that's a *new* thing for you.

Natasha: What?

Cllr: To be valued for being capable.

Natasha: Oh yes, absolutely. Whenever I've tried to be capable or achieving people have called me 'bossy' or managerial. You're not liked, you see, if you're capable. All my friends say things like 'Oh, here goes Natasha again, being bossy', or they say 'You're coming on too strong and commandeering'. I get criticisms like that, so I don't do it you see [*Natasha's bottom lip is quivering and she is close to tears again*].

At this point, the fear Natasha spoke of earlier becomes clarified and it seems to be what is preventing her from finding even a part-time job. Yet, the Capricorn process of needing to develop something in life upon which to build a specific platform *can* manifest as a managerial bossiness and control if the individual does not allow it any other channels through which to flourish. Alternatively, the individual can become the recipient of its negative manifestation in some way—having controls placed on *her* which render her oppressed (the relationship was being maintained on Peter's terms, which were limiting to Natasha; during other conversations she also mentioned situations involving her family through which controls and 'rules' were being placed upon her).

As well as transiting the MC by conjunction, ♇ also squares the natal ☉, suggesting the need for a new phase to begin. These confusing and upsetting experiences may well be 'clearing some debris' in Natasha's life so that she can achieve a positive expression of ♄ and ♇ transiting the MC—♇ also guides us to that which is held at very deep levels but which seeks to emerge into awareness. Natasha admires achieving women—she also fears being one herself. We can all be fascinated by, or detest, things in other people which we do not grant lies within ourselves. To go very deeply into these areas would be the better province of the psychotherapist, but what can the astrological counsellor do to assist the client at this point? Clearly she needs support and she is also seeking clarification.

Saturn (♄) is in the third house in Aries (♈). Saturn, the point at which we feel most vulnerable, most inferior, is in the very sign which can be drawn upon to precipitate oneself into becoming an established, flourishing and go-getting individual and in the very house through which we communicate our abilities. Saturn is in wide square to Mercury (☿) in Capricorn (♑), of which ♄ is the ruler. If this square is being lived negatively, on what does it feed? Do the current ♄ tr. and ♇ tr. (respectively the rulers of Natasha's ☉ and ☽) suggest invitations to her to begin owning her capabilities, to redeem the Competent Achieving Woman (♑ ♏), the part of her Peter validates but which she still fears? Natasha feels, even if she knows she could be achieving, that she is safer if she is not, mostly because she fears being disliked by other people. Is the ☿ □ ♄ indicative of a lifetime's belief that her abilities must be repressed, that it is wrong to be capable and achieving? And does the ☉ ☍ ♇ across the 1st/7th houses similarly suggest past experiences of domination, whereby her own creative power had little or no free rein?

All of these factors the astrological counsellor needs to be able to compute and feel into while the conversation is in process and while understanding and accepting the client's distress. To clarify some of the above, the counsellor asks Natasha to scan back over some of the times in her life she has taken initiatives or collected criticism for achieving something.

Almost immediately, Natasha recalls early factors in her life which had been half-forgotten. When she was a little girl, her mother had given birth to another child and Natasha (then aged eight) had wanted to do little things to help look after the baby. On all occasions when she tried, both her mother and a nanny they employed would tell her to go away and not to be bossy. Natasha started to uncover how a belief she developed in these early years (that she was bossy and interfering) now colours her present adult situation and she is similarly surrounding herself with people ('all my friends say . . .') who echo what she heard from her mother and the nanny.

In a short amount of work, Natasha has gone through several paths of (a) clarifying her priorities (b) looking at how she uses time (work versus being at home) (c) the main value of her relationship with Peter (d) her innate capabilities and how she has kept them in abeyance for fear of criticism which she believes she must always expect. All of these paths have value for Natasha in continuing the work so that she can eventually be in a clearer position to decide for herself what she wishes to do. In fact Natasha did continue to see the counsellor for further sessions and eventually announced that she had applied for a job with a Public Relations company ($\libra$ MC). She was successful in getting it and found that the whole company comprised herself and two bosses, both of whom positively relish Natasha's efficiency and command in organization—it was just what they were looking for! Feeling better about herself in this respect Natasha is now able to turn her attention to 'the priority' of her relationship and her own strong emotions.

Given that an overtly simple question of 'What should I do?' can hold so much within it, it becomes clear that it is wiser for the astrologer to withhold analyses and give consideration to the client's experience of her life. It would have been pointless to have hammered home to Natasha the fact that this, that and the other were transiting her chart—'good time to start a career'—'yes, go and do it'. It would not at all have served to move her any further forward in understanding herself and, in fact, may simply have reinforced and escalated her fear, as well as her belief about her supposed incapability. People are always worth more than that.

12.
CONCLUSION

There has been a cumulative need for personal counselling of many kinds and in many fields over the past decade or so. In astrology, (and as mentioned earlier in this book) this has been mirrored by many of its practitioners adjusting its traditional employment as a purely interpretational exercise. As counsellors, their ability and knowledge in chart analysis is more sensitively attuned to basic human needs and to the specific nature of their clients.

The process of astrological counselling makes searching demands upon its practitioners. Quite apart from the work involved in the calculation and consideration of a birth chart, first priorities for the counsellors are the awareness of themselves, their sensitivity, reactions, beliefs, assumptions, ability to relate and personal psychology. Just as important is the need to create a relationship with the client which is shared, rather than a solo interpretational performance on the part of the astrologer. Of course there are differences between the two people involved—the counsellor has trained and studied in astrology and counselling while the client may not have done so; but this does not make the relationship unequal; neither does it make the astrologer a super-human being. There are no perfect, totally aware astrological counsellors; they are like their clients—human beings with weaknesses and strengths, abilities and failings.

Over the years, many have arisen within the astrological profession who have made immeasurably important contributions to the psychological and spiritual understanding of astrological symbolism. Some also have specific training and experience in psychological counselling and psychotherapy, while others who wish to apply their astrological learning in this way seek such training. This can often be difficult for them, in Britain at any rate, where the opportunities for such training are not widespread. However, there are moves being made within the profession to augment this aspect of astrological work and training, whereby the astrologer may help a person take a step forward—however small—to a greater degree of self-understanding.

In the last analysis, effective counselling cannot be taught in the way that one would teach a school subject. It is a function which only through sustained practice (which may frequently be painful as the counsellor meets her limitations and blocks) enables her to acknowledge and accommodate the qualities emerging within her, which can foster an open participation with another person on his life's journey. Not all astrologers feel that they are suited to counselling—their skills lie in other applications of astrology, which are many. Others are eminently suited to it. I have been particularly aware during counselling training courses for astrologers that it is never a case of 'teaching' the astrologer 'how to be a counsellor', rather, of facilitating the emergence of the counsellor who is already there inside each person. Astrological counselling is a creative occupation that is not based on knowledge, theory or techniques, nor on 'objectivity' or that curious goal which some seek to attain, to be a 'sounding board'. As every practising counsellor knows (and perhaps from bitter as well as sweet experience), the first involvement is as a human being. Each counsellor is the foundation upon which all of the knowledge or skills ultimately rest; therefore any training begins, and continues, inside the person herself.

To the general reader or would-be client, a good place to start is to have a competent appraisal made of your birth chart. The organizations in Appendix (II) will help put you in touch with a consultant and you can ask the astrologer to explain to you his/her way of working and whether counselling and/or psychotherapeutic approaches in their astrological work are available to you if you wish. An overall discussion of your birth chart can help you both confirm things about yourself and identify those of which you may only have a diffuse knowledge and are not yet 'anchored' in your experience. It will also locate areas of your nature that you may not immediately comprehend and that may take a little while to surface into awareness. There are many levels of interpretation and the astrologer is guided to that which is relevant to you by your own cooperation and participation with her in the discussion of your life experience. Usually it is found that people can work with the material that has emerged from the initial chart discussion for quite a while after it has taken place.

Today's astrological counsellors do not contend that you of the 'unfortunate horoscope' are the hopeless victim of cosmic rays, caught up like a fly in a web, but rather that you are a person of individual potential and purpose, the outlines of which are indicated in your birth chart. The birth chart itself has been referred to by various astrological writers as a map, a blueprint, a pointer, a guide, a set of instructions from the cosmos, and a seed plan. Whichever of these words and phrases you prefer to use, they all represent the central theme of a pathway. To what use, end, fruition or goal this leads is up to the person whose central pattern of purpose this is—and who is ultimately the best person to translate it, through living it, thereby creating his or her own future.

Liz, a student in an astrology class some years ago who has done a great deal of work with it since as a guiding principle in handling and understanding her own life, has this to say:

> When I look back, where I think astrology has helped so much is that I've changed through understanding myself in a much more sure way. I'd always analysed myself deeply in every phase I've been through, but astrology has made it so much easier. What I learned from my chart instantly clarified things about myself that I'd only *thought* before, but had no real grounds to know that they were so. Take for instance all that Leo in my chart. I'd always *thought* I had it within me to be really creative and push myself forward in life, but *seeing* that in the chart, well, it was a marvellous confirmation of what was only a foggy feeling I had about myself before. Yes, that's it really. Once you can get even the basic chart factors clear, it confirms things about you; you can understand the basis of them better, and then you can start to uncover more and more about yourself that falls into place. Then you can get moving—yes, then you can move on.

While we go about the day-to-day running of our lives, there is a larger perspective for which we look concerning the nature, purpose and meaning of those lives. As a means of greater self-awareness and as an effective counselling medium, astrology has taken root to underpin the search faced by those to whom such a perspective takes a prominent place.

APPENDIX I
RECOMMENDED READING

There are literally scores of astrological books on the market, ranging from beginners' textbooks to the complex and in-depth texts. The following, however, is a short personal selection which is of value in achieving an understanding of astrology's use in counselling and as an aid to personal growth and awareness.

ARROYO, Stephen.
Astrology, Psychology and the Four Elements (CRCS Publications, 1975).
Astrology, Karma and Transformation (CRCS Publications, 1978).

CUNNINGHAM, Donna.
An Astrological Guide to Self-Awareness (CRCS Publications, 1978).

GREENE, Liz.
Relating—An Astrological Guide to Living with Others on a Small Planet (Coventure Ltd., 1977).
Saturn: A New Look at an Old Devil (Samuel Weiser Inc., New York, 1976).

MAYO, Jeff.
Astrology (Hodder & Stoughton, Teach Yourself Books, 1964).
The Planets and Human Behaviour (L. N. Fowler and Co. Ltd., 1972).

MEYER, Michael.
A Handbook for the Humanistic Astrologer (Anchor Books, 1974).

RUDHYAR, Dane.
The Astrology of Personality (first published 1936 by Lucis Publishing Company and reissued in 1963 by Servire/ Wassenaar, the Netherlands. Doubleday Paperback edition, 1970).
The Astrological Signs: The Pulse of Life (Shambhala Publications Inc., 1970).
The Practice of Astrology (first published 1968 by Servire/ Wassenaar, published in Pelican Books, 1970).
Person-Centred Astrology (ASI Publishers Inc., New York, 1980).
The Astrology of Transformation (Quest Books, The Theosophical Publishing House, U.S.A., 1980).

RUPERTI, Alexander.
Cycles of Becoming: The Planetary Pattern of Growth (CRCS Publications, 1978).

Note: The above titles published by CRCS Publications are obtainable in the U.K. through Thorsons Publishers Limited, Denington Estate, Wellingborough, Northamptonshire NN8 2RQ, or direct from CRCS in cloth and paperback editions: P.O. Box 20850, Reno, Nevada 89515, USA.

INDEX

Advice, 142, 145
Air Signs, 77-8
Alcohol, 53
Analysts, 26
Anger, 57, 116, 119
Angles, 26, 38, 51
Anxiety, 29, 124, 132
Aquarius, Age of, 25, 50
Aquarius (sign), 71, 94
Aries, 38, 61
Arroyo, Stephen, 77, 155
Ascendant, 38-40, 83
Aspects, 86-7
Astrological Association, 157

Beliefs, 39, 151
Bioenergetics, 103
Birth, 39
Birth times, 131

Cancer, 47, 52, 64
Capra, Fritjof, 20

Capricorn, 36, 38
Career, 41
Chaos, 54, 74
Characteristics, 61
Childhood, 42, 117, 118
Collusion, 58, 114
Conscience, 49
Consciousness, 9, 138
Consultants, 16
Cosmos, 20, 153
Counselling training, 27, 138, 151-2
Courage, 82, 83
Creative Journal, 103
Crises, 9, 30, 51, 82, 103, 141
Cunningham, Donna, 155
Cycles, 26, 104, 123-8

Death, 25, 56, 126
Defences, 48, 121
Depth Psychology, 24-26
Descendant, 40-1, 84

Dreams, 57, 122
Drugs, 53

Earth signs, 78
Eighth house, 85
Elements, 77
Eleventh house, 86

Fifth house, 84
Fire signs, 78-9
First house, 83
Fourth house, 84
Faculty of Astrological Studies, 157
Fate and Free Will, 31

Gemini, 39, 45, 64, 91, 92
Gestalt, 103
God, 53, 54
Greene, Liz, 40, 77, 155
Growth work, 142
Guidance, 142
Guilt, 108

Helping
  Professions, 11
Houses, 26, 81-3
Human Potential
  Resources, 158

IC, 41-2, 84, 105
Individuality, 50, 52
Insecurity, 48
Interpretation, 10,
  15-17, 24, 135-6

Jealousy, 75
Jupiter, 47-8
Jung, C. G., 20, 24

Lawrence, D. H., 51,
  54, 125, 128
Leo, 71, 110-111
Libra, 67

Marriage, 25, 40,
  109
Marriage Guidance,
  99
Mars, 16, 23, 46-7,
  58
Mayo, Jeff, 155
Mayo School of
  Astrology, 157
MC (Midheaven),
  41-2, 67, 85, 105
Mercury, 23, 44, 46,
  68
Meyer, Michael, 156
Mid-Life, 125-6
Moon, 36-8, 51
Mother, 37

Neptune, 45, 53-6
Neptune cycle, 126-7
New Age, 25, 50
Ninth house, 85

Old Age, 126

Parents, 42, 121
Pisces, 16, 46, 61,
  91
Pluto, 56-9, 71, 113
Pluto cycle, 127
Power, 58, 71
Prediction, 10,
  15-16, 102
Problems, 10, 30,
  141-3
Progressions, 26, 101
Psyche, 30
Psychodrama, 57
Psychology, 10, 49
Psychosynthesis, 103
Psychotherapy, 10,
  11, 57, 90, 152,
  103

Rage, 75
Rebellion, 51, 121
Rebirthing, 40
Rectification, 131
Rejection, 116
Retrograde motion,
  112
Rudhyar, Dane, 20,
  26, 156
Ruperti, Alexander,
  124, 127, 156

Sacrifice, 54-5, 106
Saturn, 16, 20, 23,
  45, 47, 48-9
Saturn Return, 123-4
Scorpio, 36, 39, 61,
  75
Second house, 23,
  81, 83
Seventh house, 20,
  47, 84
Singer, June, 30
Sixth house, 84, 120
Social Workers, 26
Spiritual, 53, 55

Stress, 37
Subpersonalities, 76
Suffering, 30, 49,
  118
Sun, 20, 31, 35-6,
  51
Symbols, 29-30

Taurus, 23, 46
Tenth house, 85
Therapist, 26
Third house, 83
Transactional
  Analysis, 103, 107
Transit, 104
Transpersonal
  Astrology, Centre
  for, 158
T-Square, 87, 116,
  118
Turning point, 123
Twelfth house, 86,
  91, 110

Unconscious, 26, 48,
  57, 58
Universe, 15, 19, 54,
  102
Upheaval, 56, 114,
  122
Uranus, 16, 23, 31,
  50-2, 56, 65, 67
Uranus cycle, 125

Venus, 20, 23, 44-6,
  67
Victim, 55, 153
Virgo, 36, 38, 73

Wales, HRH Prince
  of, 81
Water signs, 67, 77

Zodiac signs, 23,
  61-5

www.ingramcontent.com/pod-product-compliance
Lightning Source LLC
Chambersburg PA
CBHW071609170426

43196CB00034B/2249